The Lord is my Shepherd

"COUNTING SPOONS IS AN EMOTIONAL ROLLER COASTER RIDE THAT NEVER LETS UP. THE FIRST DIP COMES EARLY, AND HITS HARD. IT'S THAT FEELING YOU GET WHEN THE ROLLER COASTER POINTS DOWNWARD, AND YOU CAN'T HANDLE THE DROP ANY LONGER. COUNTING SPOONS JUST KEEPS GOING! WARNING: THERE MAY BE TIMES WHEN YOU CAN'T CATCH YOUR BREATH!

YOU WILL EXPERIENCE THE GRIP OF ADDICTION FROM THE PERSPECTIVE OF A MOTHER TRYING TO SAVE HER CHILD'S LIFE AND, THE SON WHO IS CHASING HIS NEXT ESCAPE FROM REALITY. IT IS GUT-WRENCHING. THIS IS A REAL, RAW, AND "IN-YOUR-FACE" JOURNEY THAT YOU WON'T SOON FORGET.

COUNTING SPOONS TAKES YOU THROUGH IT ALL: EVERY LIE, MANIPULATION, LIFE ON THE STREETS, REHAB ATTEMPTS AND RELAPSES. PUTTING THIS BOOK DOWN IS NOT AN OPTION. WILL THE FAMILY AND THOSE THAT LOVE HIM SO DEEPLY, GIVE UP ON HIM? WILL THIS DESPERATE MOM KEEP FIGHTING? WILL HER SON SURVIVE?

FOR ANYONE DEALING WITH THE MONSTER OF ADDICTION; ANYONE WHO HAS REACHED THE END OF THE ROPE AND HAS NO THREADS LEFT ON WHICH TO HANG, COUNTING SPOONS IS A STORY OF HOPE, HEALING AND FINALLY, SURRENDER TO GOD'S PLAN OF REDEMPTION.

THIS STORY WILL STAY WITH YOU FOR A VERY LONG TIME."

Wilma Hollis, Author, LifeSpeak 101: Speak Life and Win!

"ADDICTION. MOST OF US KNOW OF SOMEONE WHO HAS STRUGGLED WITH ADDICTION, BUT MANY DON'T TRULY UNDERSTAND THE STRUGGLES A FAMILY ENDURES WHEN THEY LOSE A LOVED ONE TO THIS NIGHTMARE. COUNTING SPOONS OFFERS AN UNVARNISHED LOOK AT THE VERY PERSONAL AND HEARTBREAKING 5-YEAR JOURNEY THIS FAMILY ENDURED AND PROVIDES A MESSAGE OF HOPE THROUGH LOVE, FAITH, AND RECOVERY."

Jim Rokaitis, Preventionist –Retired Police Officer

"A COMPELLING, PASSIONATE, HEARTFELT JOURNEY OF A MOTHER'S LOVE AND DETERMINATION IN FIGHTING FOR THE LIFE OF HER SON. THE IRONY OF THIS STORY IS IT'S REFLECTIVE OF THE LIVES OF SO MANY, AND YET, THE BEAUTY IS THE SAVING GRACE THROUGH JESUS CHRIST. THERE'S NO SIN, BAD HABIT, OR ADDICTION JESUS CAN'T DELIVER US FROM. COUNTING SPOONS DEMONSTRATES THE PERSEVERANCE OF A MOTHER IN PURSUIT TO SAVE THE LIFE OF HER CHILD AND FINDING JESUS, THE LIFE GIVER. I HIGHLY RECOMMEND THIS BOOK. YOU WILL BE ENCOURAGED, BLESSED, AND REMINDED "NOTHING IS TOO HARD FOR GOD"."

Rosemary McFadden, MS, LMFT, Behavioral Health Director

"IT TAKES COURAGE TO SHARE A STORY LIKE THIS, AND BOTH KATHRYN AND HER SON, JUSTIN, HAVE SHOWN EXCEPTIONAL BRAVERY. KATHRYN HAS THE UNIQUE ABILITY TO SATURATE HER WORDS WITH EMOTION - FEAR, CONFUSION, ANGER, DESPERATION. HER WORDS RESONATE WITH ME, AS THEY WILL WITH OTHER MOTHERS (FATHERS, SISTERS, BROTHERS) WHO HAVE ENDURED THE DEVASTATION OF A LOVED ONE'S DRUG OR ALCOHOL ADDICTION. BUT KATHRYN WANTS HER READERS TO KNOW THERE IS HOPE. HOPE BECAUSE WE ARE ALL GOD'S CHILDREN, AND HIS GRACE, LOVE, AND MIRACULOUS MERCY ARE THERE FOR EACH AND EVERY ONE OF US."

Sherry Randle, retired Southern Illinois Network Representative of SCBWI (Society of Children's Book Writers and Illustrators)

"A MUST READ...COUNTING SPOONS WILL TAKE YOU ON AN INTIMATELY PERSONAL TOUR DEEP INSIDE THE DARK AND DEPRAVED HEART OF ADDICTION. THIS AUTHENTIC, VULNERABLE, AND TOUCHING STORY TRULY REVEALS THE DECEITFULNESS OF THE HUMAN HEART AND MANKIND'S DESPERATE NEED FOR THE INTERVENTION OF A GRACIOUS GOD BRINGING RESCUE TO THE LOST THROUGH HIS SON, JESUS CHRIST. NOT ONLY WILL MANY RELATE TO THIS STORY, BUT I WOULD GUARANTEE MOST WILL FIND HOPE AND THE ANSWERS THEY'VE BEEN LOOKING FOR IN THEIR SEARCH FOR FREEDOM FROM THE ENSLAVEMENT OF ADDICTION.

'IF THE SON SETS YOU FREE THEN YOU ARE FREE INDEED' – JOHN 8:36."

Oliver Underwood - ACBC/CABC/TAC Northwest Regional Coordinator

"COUNTING SPOONS IS A STORY THAT RESONATES AND STAYS WITH YOUR SOUL. IT HAS CHANGED MY PERSPECTIVE AND IT DAILY REMINDS ME TO SEE THE HOPE IN THOSE WHO ARE STRUGGLING. THIS MEMOIR IS AN HONEST ACCOUNT OF LIFE, LOVE, ADDICTION, AND THE POWER OF FAITH. I AM A BETTER PERSON FOR READING IT."

Morgan Rossiter, Educator and Mother

"THE BEAUTY OF "COUNTING SPOONS" IS IN THE PERSPECTIVE – OF KATHRYN, A FIERCELY LOVING AND HEADSTRONG MOTHER, AND JUSTIN, HER YOUNGEST SON ENSNARED BY HEROIN USE. EACH TELLS A STORY OF LIFE IN ADDICTION THROUGH THEIR OWN LENS, GIVING US A UNIQUE GLIMPSE INTO THE EVENTS THAT CHALLENGED AND CHANGED THEM FOREVER. ALTHOUGH THEIR STORIES TAKE ON A DIFFERENT TRAJECTORY, THEY RECONNECT AT THE END THANKS TO GREAT HOPE, FAITH, RENEWED TRUST, AND REDEMPTION – AND AN UNWAVERING DEVOTION TO GOD."

Lori Schumacher, Program Director - Former Deputy Probation Officer

"IF YOU LOVE AN ADDICT OR ARE WALKING ALONGSIDE SOMEONE WHO IS STRUGGLING WITH ADDICTION, THIS BOOK IS FOR YOU. IF YOU NEED HOPE, A LIGHT AT THE END OF A VERY DARK TUNNEL, THIS BOOK IS FOR YOU. THE AUTHOR INVITES YOU INTO HER PERSONAL JOURNEY TO SAVE HER SON FROM HIS HEROIN ADDICTION. HER WRITING IS INTIMATE AND RAW AS SHE SHARES HER DESPERATION, HELPLESSNESS, ISOLATION, AND PAIN. BUT MOST IMPORTANTLY, SHE SHARES THE HOPE SHE FOUND WHEN SHE SURRENDERED CONTROL TO HER LORD AND SAVIOR JESUS CHRIST. IT'S A PAINFUL, YET BEAUTIFUL STORY OF REDEMPTION, GRACE, AND TRANSFORMATION. READ THIS BOOK AND THEN SHARE IT WITH SOMEONE WHO NEEDS HOPE. GOD WILL DO THE REST!"

Cindy Duenas, MFT, Executive Director

A MEMOIR OF HEROIN, HEARTACHE, AND HOPE

Counting Spoons

A MEMOIR OF HEROIN, HEARTACHE, AND HOPE

Counting Spoons

BY KATHRYN MAE INMAN

Arabelle Publishing, LLC, Chesterfield, VA

Counting Spoons
A MEMOIR OF HEROIN, HEARTACHE, AND HOPE
Copyright© 2022 Kathryn Mae Inman

Published by Arabelle Publishing, LLC
Chesterfield, VA 23832
www.arabellebooks.com
IG: @arabellepublishing

Unless otherwise indicated, all Scripture quotations are taken from the Holy Bible, New Living Translation, copyright© 1996, 2004, 2015 by Tyndale House Foundation. Used by permission of Tyndale House Publishers, Carol Stream, Illinois 60188, USA. All rights reserved.

The events and dialogue in this story are based on the author's memory. We have changed some of the names of characters to safeguard the privacy of the individuals.

Cover design by Samuel Rog
Interior design by Julie Basinski

Composition/Song Title: Death Was Arrested
Copyright © 2015 Centricity Songs (BMI) BCoker Music (BMI) Adam Kersh Music (BMI) Paul Taylor Smith Publishing (BMI) (adm. at CapitalCMGPublishing.com) All rights reserved. Used by permission.

Library of Congress Control Number: 2021952094

ISBN: 978-1-7356328-5-8
Printed in the United States of America
10 9 8 7 6 5 4 3 2 1
First Paperback Edition

THIS BOOK IS DEDICATED TO

The Lord Jesus Christ
All the glory unto Him

"AND SHE LOVED THE LITTLE BOY VERY, VERY MUCH.
EVEN MORE THAN SHE LOVED HERSELF."

Shel Silverstein

TABLE OF CONTENTS

PROLOGUE
INTRODUCTION *We Will Do This Together*

ACKNOWLEDGMENTS

TO MY HUSBAND, thank you for your support and patience as I threw myself into writing this book. Thank you for taking me to a beautiful island so I could draw closer to the Lord, and thank you for loving me with your whole heart. You are my always and forever. I love you madly.

TO MY SISTER MARTHA, thanks for tolerating my craziness as I wrote. I'm pretty sure I freaked out daily, and you always reassured or ignored me; both responses worked! Thank you for your support, guidance, spirit, love, tolerance, and for knowing me better than I know myself. You are brilliant and made my writing come to life. I could not have done it without you. Love you so much.

TO MY WARRIOR SISTERS, Cindy, Rosemary, Valerie, and Kristen. Thank you for your prayers, encouragement, patience, and most of all, your love. You are such a beautiful example of godly women. I love you.

TO ALL MY FAMILY, and to the Fahey, Rossiter, Butson, Copra, Lambert, Schumacher, Huckaby, Camacho, Underwood, Nadykto, and CHS families. To Dawn Heather and Kyle, Blake, Chad, Tiffany, and to all who read and gave feedback on my manuscript—thank you. There are many times I rested on the shoulders of your love, even when you didn't know it. I love you guys.

TO JUSTIN'S WASHINGTON PARENTS, John, and Fran. I don't know what we would have done without you. I'll never forget when John drove across three states to pick up Justin after court and take him back to Washington, and how Fran answered every one of my frantic phone calls. Fran, you always knew what to say and I thank you for that. Christ shines brightly in you both. We love you!

TO JOHNNIE PHILLIPS, I am ever-so-grateful that God led me to you that day at Big Valley Grace, when I was so broken and desperate. You walked this journey with us, gave me hope, prayed, and answered every one of my phone calls. Thank you, Johnnie, for EVERYTHING. May God bless and keep you.

TO BRIAN RALSTON, thank you for all you have done for our family. We are so blessed by you! You will forever be my favorite pastor and fly brother-in-Christ. We love you!

TO MY EDITOR, Rick Steele, thank you for walking me through this writing journey. Your feedback inspired me to keep going! May God bless you, always.

TO MY SWEET COUSIN, beta-reader, sister-in-Christ, and friend, Sherry Randle. Thank you. I adore you.

TO SHAYLIN NICOLE, I treasure memories of you as a little girl, taking long walks together with you sitting in your red wagon. Watching you become a big sister to your brothers was the sweetest gift. You taught me what love is and my world is so much more beautiful with you in it. God knows I love you!

TO MY OLDEST SON, Dillon. Thank you for your strength! I don't think I could have survived the struggle without you. You are such a joy in my life. Your honesty, love, encouragement, and confidence lifted me up as I was writing. Always know how much I love you! May you continue your walk-in faith and be blessed abundantly in Christ.

TO JUSTIN. This is it, Son! Our journey and the miracles and blessings from the Lord captured in these pages. Thank you for inspiring me every day, and for the example you set as someone who puts Christ first. We survived the darkness and, as hard as it was, I thank God because He brought us right where we are supposed to be. I praise Him for His kindness and the abundance of grace and mercy that covers our growing family. Always know I love you, and how proud I am to be your mom. He reigns!

TO KAYLEIGH AND LANE, you bless our family richly. May your life together be all you've dreamed of. Love you so much!

TO JUSTIN ANTHONY, I have loved you from the start. May God bless and keep you.

TO AMANDA GRACE AND JESSICA ANN. The beauty you both add to our family is immeasurable. Such strong and amazing women; we are so blessed by you! Love you both.

TO MOM, DAD, MY BROTHER RANDY, AND FATHER-IN-LAW DON—thank you for sending me love and strength from His Kingdom above. I will see you again when I am finally called home. I love you!

AND TO OUR PRECIOUS GRANDDAUGHTER, Everly Grace. You, my love, are such a light and joy to our family, and I love you more than you will ever know. I cannot wait to see what God has in store for you in His kingdom. May you always be strong, fear the Lord, know love in abundance and, my darling girl, be fierce!

TO SWEET JEREMIAH DEAN, our first grandson. Every time I look into your bright blue eyes, all I can think of is that God dropped a sparkle of the summer sky in your baby blues so we could get a tiny glimpse of heaven. Whatever you grow up to be, I know you will be magnificent. Love you.

AND FINALLY, OUR THIRD GRANDCHILD and second grandson, Ledger McKnight. This book was finished before you were even thought of, but somehow I've held you in my heart for many years. May you grow to be courageous, kind, and strong. I love you, Ledge.

TO ARABELLE PUBLISHING, thank you for taking a chance on us! I am so grateful God led me to you.

PROLOGUE

Our story is not just about addiction, it's about second chances and living a life of freedom. It's based on a true story about our family and our youngest son, Justin. He had everything going for him, but he was empty inside. He was searching for something to fill a need, and that search led him on a downward spiral of crime and addiction, living on the streets, and strung out on heroin. In the pages that follow, you will hear about our journey from both mine and Justin's perspectives.

I hope the information in this book is helpful and can ease the hurt of others going through addiction with a loved one. Sometimes we find comfort just knowing we are not alone in our suffering.

You'll find my heart in this book! If you decide to turn the next pages, I pray it brings you something. Clarity? A stirring of the Lord? Hope? Belief that redemption is real? I just long for it to bring you something meaningful. For me, long after this writing collects dust, I will continue to rejoice in the Lord. My hope and strength lie in Him and that will always be enough.

Content Warning: This book contains sensitive content related to substance abuse and addiction. Drug use is described in a tone that may distress the reader, as if it takes pain away and brings comfort from suffering. It produces horrific pain. Our intention is to parallel the pain associated with drug abuse and the insidious lure of pleasure that sadly traps so many. It is important to note the dangers. Many first-time users accidentally overdose and die, and some people become addicted after using drugs only one time. According to the Addiction Center, approximately 2.1 million Americans have an opioid addiction and about 130 deaths from opioid overdose occur every day. Statistics on deaths related to heroin and fentanyl use are even more alarming. If you or a loved one needs help related to substance abuse and addiction, please contact your local Behavioral Health or Social Services Department to find support and resources near you. We also encourage you to reach out to your local church.

INTRODUCTION

KATHRYN

A few years after what I refer to as the "dark times," when my son was active in his addiction, God placed it in my heart to put my thoughts on paper. A book? Perhaps, or maybe a journal. Maybe family would read it, or no one would. I didn't really care. With no expectation, I started pouring out what was on my heart into pages on my laptop.

After I started writing and with several years of sobriety under his belt, my youngest son, Justin, came from Washington to visit our home in California. I was about ten pages in and, because I was writing about our journey as mother and son, it was important to me that he was comfortable with the content and that he supported the idea of me writing our story. Other than my sister, I had let no one read my work, so this was kind of a big deal.

Early one morning when just he and I were awake, I got my coffee, checked my ego, and gave Justin what I had written. I walked outside to the back patio to give him some space and privacy as he read, and I waited. It felt like I was waiting a long time. I wandered back into the house and walked by Justin, but he didn't look up; he was still reading. I noticed he had an indifferent look on his face, and I started thinking that this may have been a bad idea. I could feel my heart pounding, and suddenly realized how much this meant to me. I refilled my cup and went back outside and waited.

After what felt like an eternity, Justin came out and took a seat in the chair next to mine, but he was not looking at me. I tried to pace myself, because I'm known for asking too many questions of my children. I waited in silence for a bit, and then he finally started talking. He declared that "If this book or whatever it is, is going to happen, then it has to be real and full of truth." Justin had passion in his voice, and I could see the veins in his neck pulsing. Was he mad? Did I misrepresent things? Was this too soon to revisit the painful memories? Justin continued... he talked about life on the streets, the darkness, and the ugliness of it all. He told me that "Nothing can be sugar coated; all of it has to be captured as raw and painful as that might be." A wave of fear rushed over me as I realized there was still so much I didn't know.

Justin emphasized the importance of truth, of glorifying the Lord in all our words. He said, "If we don't accomplish that, then we have no business writing. The purpose is to help others and spread a message of hope, right?" He looked at me, and I nodded my head. I agreed with everything he was saying. It was quiet for a few minutes. I felt nervous and my thoughts were scattered. I closed my eyes, trying to clear my head and asked him, "Should I even be doing this?" He took a breath, exhaled, and a slow grin spread across his face.

> ## YES, MOM, IT'S GOOD.
> ## THIS IS A GOOD IDEA.
> ## LET'S DO IT TOGETHER.

I resisted the urge to jump up and thrust my fist in the air. Instead, I calmly sat in my chair and continued to sip my coffee. It was then that I felt the sudden sting of tears in my eyes and the weight of a heavy lump in my throat. We would do this together? Yes, we would. We certainly would.

"I'VE LEARNED NOW THAT WHILE THOSE WHO SPEAK
ABOUT ONE'S MISERIES USUALLY HURT, THOSE
WHO KEEP SILENCE HURT MORE."

C.S. Lewis

Counting Spoons

24

GOING NOWHERE

CHAPTER

ONE

JUSTIN 2015

Heroin makes me feel like a whole person. From the first time I got high and floated into that warm, brown haze, I knew I had finally found what I'd been chasing. I've always been the guy that will try anything and everything for a good time and when I first tried heroin, I knew my search was over; I'd finally found the ultimate high. I mean, it was like I met a new lover. I picture heroin like a seductive woman; my body aches for her, and I can't get enough. If I'm not high, I'm thinking about being high and I pursue her all day, every day.

I want to shout out to all of you at home that believed in me. I'm sorry! I'm sorry I'm such a disappointment and not the strong guy you thought I was. I'm weak behind this drug; I admit it! I know it's bad and has ruined just about everything good in my life, but I can't stop. I've tried countless times, and I always go back to it.

I left my family back in Modesto because I had to. Everyone was looking for me, and I ripped off a lot of people, so it was time to move on. I miss them and think about them a lot, but I can't go back; they don't understand who I really am. I still love my family and friends, and I hate what I've done to them, but it's not enough to stop me. At least now that I'm away, they're protected from me. My mom changed the locks to keep me out of the house, so I guess I'm doing everyone a favor. I'm living on the streets, in one of the worst neighborhoods in Oakland, free to do as I please with no one breathing down my neck.

We're running out of dope; it's time to make some money. Eric and I have a routine; we shoot heroin during the day and shoot crystal meth at night. If I'm going to get sleep, it's gotta be during the day. You do not close your eyes at night on the streets where I'm living. You'll get jumped, robbed, and maybe even killed if you do. During the day, we steal whatever we can, cash it in with our contact, get money, buy our dope and then we party through the night and do it all over again the next day. I don't know exactly how long I've been here, but it's been a while.

I remember when I first came to the Bay Area. We got a ride, checked into some raunchy rehab place, and I left within a few hours. I had some money come in and paid my buddy to pick me up and take me back to Modesto. I got a bunch of dope, checked into a hotel room, and lived large for two days, and when the drugs ran out, I got a ride back. Initially, I came back to Oakland to get clean. I checked into detox, but three days later I was kicked out after the staff found needles in my bag. The funny thing is, I didn't even know the needles were in there! My buddy, Eric, didn't want to leave me hanging, so he walked out of detox right after me. We made our way to 73rd and International in East Oakland hoping to find some dope. We were both dope sick, and the withdrawals were hitting us hard, but we kept moving. I gotta say, I felt like a fish out of water. I was a white guy in an area where there weren't many, and I stuck out like a sore thumb. Initially it was rough, and I had a lot to figure out, but I ended up finding a good dope connection, and despite how bad my surroundings were, I couldn't think of any reason to leave. I had everything I needed, so I stayed.

I'll never forget my first night in Oakland. Eric kept telling me we couldn't be on the streets at night, or we would get jumped. We had no money and no place to go, so I called around trying to get someone to pay for a hotel room for me, but no one would do it. I had really burned my bridges back home. I was desperate and scared and didn't know anything about this way of life. Before, I always had a money source, a car, and friends in the area, but not here. We ended up staying under a bridge behind some bushes and I didn't sleep a wink; I was terrified.

But things are different now; I'm comfortable here and know people on every block. I can handle myself with just about anyone. I'm a lot thinner and weaker than I used to be, but I can still fight, and I'll do whatever I need to do to survive. I've been in and out of jail, and the cops know me; they're always hassling me, but I manage it. I'm finding my way and getting good at this new life.

My mom would freak out if she knew how I was living; it's better for her to believe whatever it is that she believes. She couldn't handle seeing me like this, and I don't want her to; the less she knows the better. I don't want my family around me anymore. Everything is different now.

It's time to start moving. It takes me about an hour to hit Bargain Mart, Lenny's Drugstore, and the Value Shop. I find a trash bag behind a dumpster and throw in what I stole; two boxes of Rogaine®, five boxes of Crest ®White Strips, fifteen tubes of anti-aging cream, and fifteen boxes of Claritin®and Zyrtec®, 80 count. A lot of these products have security magnets, so I made sure that I walked in the store with a magnet so the alarm would go off. That way they wouldn't be suspicious when the alarm went off as I was leaving with stolen merchandise; it works every time. I look at what I lifted and try to add up the value in my head, but I can't seem to think straight. I tell myself it will be enough and tuck the bag into the front of my coat and zip it up. I hop on BART (Bay Area Rapid Transit) from Union City and head back to Oakland. I walk two long miles to my contact on 96th Avenue and she cashes me out handing me $215.00. My feet are hurting so I stop and kick off my old Converses with no laces and slowly peel off my sock. I'm holding my breath because it hurts, and I want to scream. I have sores that won't heal, and my socks are sticking to the raw skin on the bottom of my feet. I feel like crying, but I need to keep moving because nothing will hurt in about twenty minutes. I walk sixteen blocks to my dealer, and I'm relieved to see him, he's always there. I slip him two hundred bucks, and he gives me twenty balloons of dope; ten bags of heroin, and ten bags of crystal meth. Now I'm set for another night.

I have a little cash left, so I walk to the corner store and grab a Snickers® bar, a bottle of water, and a mint ice cream sandwich. You know, the kind that's an ice cream sandwich dipped in chocolate? I eat them whenever I can find them because they're delicious. I devour my candy bar, chug some water, and plop down next to the dumpster.

A grungy looking kitten comes around the corner and looks at me. He's gray and black striped with a pink nose. I coax him over to give him some of my ice cream and he laps it up. His eyes meet mine, and we stare at each other until he blinks and then I hear him purring. "Hey little buddy, why are you out here all alone?" I pour some of my water on the ground and he laps that up too. He jumps on my leg, curls up against me and I love him already. Maybe we'll stick together and he'll be my cat. I pick him up and tuck him inside my coat, and quietly promise to look out for him.

I can't remember when I slept last, and my eyes feel heavy. I find an old blanket someone left and decide to lay down for just a few minutes, and then I completely black out.

I wake to the sound of something banging. I look up and see an old homeless man yelling and hitting a pan against the cyclone fence, and I want him to stop; just please stop! I can't handle the noise. I sit up and try to collect my thoughts. My head is pounding, and I'm sick. I feel it coming and roll over in time to puke on the sidewalk. I keep puking until the wretched bile comes up. I'm gagging so hard I feel like I'm going to cough up my liver or lungs or something. Man, I feel like death, and I need water. I'm sweating, and my mouth is so dry I feel like I can't swallow. I black out again and wake up to the sun going down. I wonder how many hours I've been asleep and can't figure out if it's even the same day. I've got to pull myself together. I remember the kitty and look around in a panic, but he's long gone.

I get to my feet and check my pockets, only to find them empty. I have no money or dope left. I brush myself off and pull out my toothbrush and toothpaste and start brushing as best I can without water. I spit out the paste and throw-up again. I wipe my mouth with my sleeve and will myself to start moving. I need to get high, and I need to find a phone.

I get to my dealer, and he fronts me some because he knows I'm good for it. He laughs at how bad I look, "Rough night, dude?" I don't even look up when I tell him to get lost. He's a piece of crap anyway. I duck behind the bridge, get my rig out, and inject the brown serum into my veins. My eyes get heavy as I lean my head back against the fence, letting the sweet sensation spread slowly through my arms and legs; it coats my stomach and eases everything. Within seconds I almost feel good again. I slowly exhale and feel the relief cover my entire body. I tell myself everything is going to be okay. I wish I could find kitty again, and decide I'll go back to the store later and look for him.

I walk towards the strip mall and grocery stores to start hustling and notice an older lady that seems to be struggling with her grocery bags. I jog up and ask if she needs help, and she does. I load them in her trunk and close it for her. She's about the same age my grandma was when she passed away. Short and plump, with thick gray hair piled up on top of her head in a bun, and she smells like musky perfume. She thanks me for helping, and I ask if I can use her phone to call my mom.

"Of course dear, take your time." I open the door for her, and she gets in the driver's seat. I tell her I'll just be a few minutes. I hold the phone in my hand and stare at it. The idea of stealing it crosses my mind, but it's just a fleeting thought; instinctive I guess, but I don't take it. When I left Modesto, I decided that I was going to stop stealing from people, and only steal from businesses. I realize this makes me more of a criminal, but I also think it makes me less of a punk.

I walk to the front of her car, lean on the hood, and call my mom. She still has the same number; it's one of the many phone numbers I have etched in my brain. Her voice calms me; it sounds like home and makes me feel like a little kid again.

"Hi Justin, talk to me." I tell her I'm fine and on a waiting list for a program. I ask about my brother, Dillon, and our dog, Maggie, and she tells me they're doing well. She updates me on my sister, Shay, and says Aunt Martha asked about me.

"You should see the sunset here, Mom, it's beautiful. I had a good day; didn't do much, just hung out with some friends." I answer a few questions; *yes, I have a place to sleep... yes, I'm eating and drinking...*

And then she starts in, "Are you getting tired yet, Justin? Aren't you getting tired of this life you're living?" —that's my cue to say goodbye.

"Hey, I gotta go, bye Mom, I love you! I'll call you tomorrow."

"OK, Justin, keep calling. I love you and I hate this! I'll keep praying for you."

I wish I would have hung up sooner. I don't want to think about her praying for me. I don't want to think about my brother, or my dog, or any of that stuff. It's just easier to forget about them. I hang up and give the sweet old lady her phone back, and she asks if everything is okay. I gulp down the lump in my throat, tap on the hood of her car, and tell her "Yep, never been better!" I do my best to smile, and head back out to nowhere.

KATHRYN 2015

It's been a few days since I've heard from him, and I'm sick with worry. My heart hurts: it's like there's a heavy weight on my chest, and I can't get enough air into my lungs. He usually calls me every day. I don't know why he calls, or how he finds a phone, but he always does, and I'm grateful for that—because it's the only way I know he's still alive.

My mind starts reeling; maybe he's not alive. Maybe he overdosed and he's out there dead somewhere. He has no identification on him, so they wouldn't know who he is or where he's from. The thought brings on a wave of anxiety, and I feel like I'm going to lose it. If he is dead, how will I ever know? If I don't hear from him by tomorrow, then I'll know something bad has happened, and I'll need to go look for him, but I have no idea where he is. I know he's in a bad part of Oakland, and even though I grew up in the area, I don't know enough about the city to know where the bad neighborhoods are. I have no idea where I would even begin to look for him. I try to calm down and focus on breathing.

My sister, Martha, calls and picks up on my mood.

"What's wrong?"

I tell her nothing, really.

"Nope, I don't believe you, what is it?

I explain that I haven't heard from Justin in three days.

"Kathy, you have to stop doing this. You need to tell him to get into treatment or stop calling you! Every time he misses a day you think he's dead and honestly, at this point I'm more worried about you than him."

I listen but don't respond. I know she's right but what am I supposed to do? I can't stop my thoughts, and no matter what he's done, he is still my son.

Martha continues "So how are you getting by, what are your days like?"

I tell her they're all the same, I just do my thing; she asks me to be more specific.

"Well, I just take one step at a time. I wake up and tell myself to get up, then I tell myself to get in the shower, then to brush my teeth, I mean I just focus on breathing and whatever task is next, and then the next one, and the next one, and next one. I just keep doing that throughout my day."

There's silence on the phone and then Martha responds, "Wow, okay, that's really weird. You tell yourself out loud what you need to do all day, like one thing at a time?" I laugh because she sounds so serious.

"Yep, that's what I do, I'm fine, really, for some reason it just helps me." She's not laughing. "You know you can't go on like this, right? This is going to kill you if you don't get some help."

I don't like how serious she sounds, and I don't want to talk about this right now. I tell her I must go and promise to call back later.

I kicked Justin out of the house a few months ago because I had to; too much has happened. He needs to figure this out on his own, but honestly, I did not expect it to go this way. It's been months now, and he's still out there. I expected him to hit rock bottom quickly, but now I feel like he's getting used to life on the streets. I worry that he's forgetting who he really is! As far as I know, he never comes back into town, and he doesn't ask for anything, so I wonder how he's getting money. I know he's using, and his habit is expensive. I expect that he'll end up in jail, and I'm hoping that will finally be his "rock bottom."

I still can't believe he relapsed again, but this time it's so much worse. I wonder if he's beyond hope. Is he just too deep into this that he can't ever pull himself out? Martha's right, I have to stop thinking this way and I need to get a handle on things.

On just three hours of sleep, I manage to get through the day. I go to work and focus on the tasks in front of me; keeping my phone close in case he calls, but he doesn't. At 5:00, I change into my workout clothes, and instead of going to the gym, I go to the track and run the bleachers. It helps me blow off some energy and I feel better. My boyfriend is out of town on business, and my oldest son is out of state playing baseball, so I have the house to myself and I'm grateful for that. I don't want to be around anyone right now. I just want Justin to call so I know he's still alive.

I pull in the garage, grab my stuff out of the back seat, step into the house, and then I hear my phone ring. Crap! It's in the car! Okay, drop everything, okay, run to the car, okay, now get your phone and look at it, okay, keep breathing . . . that's not a number I know; keep breathing; please let it be him, just keep breathing. . . .

"Hello?" I'm holding my breath and then I hear it.

"Hey, Mom!" Relief comes like a tidal wave. I drop to the floor and close my eyes, willing my pounding heart to slow down. He's alive. I lean back against the garage door and try to calm down; he's okay, he's alive.

"Hi Justin, talk to me." He tells me the same things he always tells me. He's on a waiting list for a program, he's doing well, he's sleeping at a friend's house, he's gaining weight, *blah blah blah.* I guess he thinks I believe him, but I don't. I hear the crack and strain in his voice, and I know he's high. It's hard not to react in anger because hearing him high turns me completely inside out, but I'm so relieved he's alive that I'm not going to say a word about it today. He's heard it all from me before, and it doesn't seem to matter anyway. I focus on keeping my voice strong and steady, and try not to ask too many questions.

He's living a nightmare; I know he is, and it's his choice. After two years of being clean, at some point he decided to go back down this road that ends in misery and despair. It has happened every single time he has committed to getting clean. But this relapse is the worst and makes all the other times pale in comparison. When we talk, he tries to make it sound like everything is fine, but he's not doing well. When I think about how he's poisoning his body and the conditions he's probably living in, it sickens me.

I keep the conversation going as long as I can and then ask, "Are you done yet, Justin? Aren't you tired of living this life?" He quickly cuts me off. I tell him I'll be praying and want him to keep calling. He ends the conversation and hangs up, but not before telling me he loves me and I love him too, I really do. He's my son, and I'm not giving up on him, but my hope is dwindling. I did everything I could to help him get healthy and it didn't work, so now he's on his own. I can't have him in my life when he's using. He's not allowed back in our home, but when he's ready to go into treatment, I'll be there. I just hope someday I'll get my son back—because I don't know who this person is. The Justin I raised is kind and loving. The addicted Justin is not someone I want to be around. He lies and steals and only cares about one thing and that's getting high.

I flash back to his Junior year in High School. Justin was going to the senior prom with a girl that he was dating, and he was excited about it. He had his hair fixed just right with his brown curls falling around his face, and his lean, muscular body filled out his tuxedo perfectly. He splashed on just a little too much cologne, and his dress shoes were polished and shiny. He had gas in his tank, a little money in his wallet, and a beautiful, white corsage that he picked out to give his date. He was ready! He checked himself in the mirror a few times and then came out to the living room with a big grin on his face. He flexed and posed and then jumped right in front of me.

"Mom! How do I look?"

"You look handsome, Son."

And he did; he was beaming. I heard him on the phone with his date, "Hey, come now because I want to stop by my grandma's so she can see us." He hangs up, and I ask him about it. He tells me he talked to his grandma earlier, and she was going to play bingo in the hall, so he wanted to surprise her and walk in when she was surrounded by her friends. My mom often bragged about her grandkids, and I knew she would be thrilled. He giggles. "She's going to be so surprised, Mom. You should come with us!" I grabbed my camera and followed them. It was one of those moments you just never forget; my mom's face lit up as soon as she saw her handsome grandson walking up in his tuxedo with a pretty girl on his arm. I watch as Justin wraps his arms around his Grandma, hugging her tightly. They didn't stay long; they didn't need to. My mom would talk about this day for months to come.

At Justin's request his date takes a picture of us. He drapes his arm across my shoulders and smiles wide for the camera. I pull him

33

aside and start in, "Son, do not stay out late, you need to be home by midnight and do not drink! Be a gentleman and have fun, just be careful." I look at him and realize he had stopped listening a while ago and was just standing there smiling, waiting for me to finish.

"You done, Mom?"

"Yes, Son, I'm done. Have fun, okay?"

"Yep!"

He hugs me tight and then takes off to catch up to his date. I hang out for a few minutes and watch them. He runs up behind her and scoops her into his arms and twirls her around. I see their smiles and hear their giggles, and I'm reminded of the excitement and beauty of young love. He gets her settled in the passenger seat, shuts her door, and turns back in my direction one last time. He waves and yells from across the parking lot, "Love you, Mom!" He hops in, and they drive away with the music blaring so loud I'm certain my mom and her friends can hear it. I remember smiling the whole way home.

Justin Dean was a sweet and loving young man and then everything changed. Before I even knew what hit us, he was deep in his addiction, and I felt like he was a total stranger. I don't like this Justin. I don't trust him, and I feel like he's capable of most anything. This is not the son I raised! Justin is a heroin addict living on the streets, and there's not a thing I can do about it. I wonder for the millionth time how we ended up in this miserable place. Sometimes I don't think I can take it anymore, but the days keep coming and going. He's still out there on the street doing God knows what, and I'm still here with shattered nerves and a heaviness in my chest. I tell myself, breathe, okay, breathe again, just keep breathing, but I feel like I'm drowning. Talking to myself doesn't really work because my heart races all the time. I'm in a constant state of anxiety because I know I'm losing my son, and I'm not sure how I'm going to live in this world without him.

"I'VE ALWAYS LOVED BUTTERFLIES,
BECAUSE THEY REMIND US THAT
IT'S NEVER TOO LATE TO
TRANSFORM OURSELVES."

Drew Barrymore

Counting Spoons

FROM THE BEGINNING

CHAPTER
TWO

KATHRYN

He was born on March 31, 1993. The doctor and three sonograms told us it was a girl, but Justin Dean Usiak was *all boy*. I remember the look on everyone's face as they heard the news that the precious little girl we were expecting was an 8lb, 9oz, 21-inch beautiful baby boy. My sweet stepdaughter, Shaylin (we call her Shay), was eight years old at the time, and by the look on her face I thought she might cry at the news that another brother was coming home with us, as she was fully prepared for a little sister. On the other hand, my first-born son, Dillon, who was three years old, was thrilled that he would have a brother to play with. Justin was brought into the world surrounded by family that loved him very much.

Justin was an easy, happy child. He loved being around people and was affectionate with a sweet disposition. He was always on the go and had endless energy and enthusiasm for life in general. You couldn't help but notice his smile and big brown eyes that seemed to sparkle with mischief. He always had that look about him, like he was about to get into something. He grew from the newborn with a swollen face and a shock of dark hair, to a towheaded boy with big brown eyes, to the teenager that hit puberty like a rocket launching into outer space. Watching Justin grow up was like watching a movie where you find yourself sitting on the edge of your seat, trying to anticipate what might happen next. From a toddler to a young adult, Justin was larger than life and seemed to always be looking for the next big adventure.

Justin was a good student who gradually turned into a mediocre student. He enjoyed the social aspect of school much more than the academic part. He didn't want to read, hated sitting still for homework, and made sure to participate in every sports event, spirit rally, and social activity he could. Teachers seemed to really take to him, or they were irritated by him, and he usually felt the same. If he sensed they didn't like him he would shut down or intentionally misbehave. He wasn't interested in repairing relationships and seemed to get underneath the skin of some of his teachers. I remember feeling taken aback by their comments about how unruly Justin could be. They either loved him, or they couldn't seem to tolerate him; there wasn't much in-between.

The divorce was rough. Justin was just three years old and doesn't have memories of his father and me together, but as he got older, he would get really uncomfortable being in the same room with us. He could feel the tension that always seemed to hover around our family.

As a kid, Justin was a bundle of energy and what you would call "a handful". He lacked self-control from a very young age. He was lean but muscular, with big hands to go along with an explosive temper. His first knockout was at an all-star baseball game in Turlock, California. He was eight years old. He skateboarded to the corner market to get some sunflower seeds between games. From what the store clerk told me, a tall, lanky, boy about 18-19 years old tried to take his money, and before the clerk could get around the counter, Justin swung hard, hitting him in the jaw, and down he went; knocked out cold with a bloody nose. The clerk made Justin get me, and by the time I arrived, the kid he hit had come to and run home; a pool of blood and my son's swollen knuckles were the only evidence that the fight had happened. Justin had a definite sense of right and wrong, and if someone tried to wrong him, he wasn't going to take it without a fight.

I remember things usually came easily to Justin. So it surprised me when he came home one afternoon upset from the day he had while in grade school. He was asked to give an oral presentation in front of the class, and he couldn't do it, so he got an "incomplete." He walked in the door and was anxious to tell me what happened "Mom, I choked, I just couldn't do it!"

"Well, Justin Dean, what are you going to do about it?"

He decided he was not only going to give a presentation, but he was going to give an amazing one. He stayed up late that night preparing, and the next day when he returned to class, he asked for another chance. This time he delivered a strong presentation and landed an A. He would go on to become the class vice president and in sixth grade, won a speech contest. Justin rarely encountered things he couldn't do, but when he did, he would figure out a way to make it happen. Failure didn't seem to be an option for him.

When I first realized Justin was doing drugs, it horrified me. I learned a lot through Justin's journey. The most important is that God is good and in control. Here are some of the other things I learned from having a son addicted to drugs:

- You can truly hate someone you love
- Lack of sleep and stress can make you crazed and irrational
- Jack in the Box will give water to homeless people
- You can sell anything at a pawn shop, no questions asked
- Tough love is necessary
- Isolation is not a good thing
- You are not responsible for the actions of your addicted family member
- You should never pay their debts
- Always sleep with your purse/wallet by your pillow

I compared Justin to a hyena in the wilderness; a hunched over scavenger lurking in the dark waiting for scraps. That's what I used to think of my son; I felt like this beautiful child had turned into an evil monster. I prayed that the addiction would leave his body and come into mine. That may sound heroic, but it wasn't at all. Watching my son destroy himself was the most painful thing I've ever been through, and I knew if the addiction were in me, I could get through it somehow and, if it was in me then I would have control again.

It bothered me that Justin had an out. He would do drugs and numb himself to the pain, but nothing numbed me. I couldn't escape the heartache, ever. It was present, like a heavy, dark cloud that followed me around every minute of my day. So how did I cope? I buried it inside me. I stopped being social. I went to work every day and worked hard. I functioned as normally as I could and avoided anything that made me uncomfortable. I wasn't eating; at 5'7" my healthy weight is around 135 pounds. I got down to just under 120, and with the lack of sleep I looked every bit as worn as I felt.

I remember looking in the mirror and telling myself I had to get it together. I would tell myself to stop acting crazy. *Do not let this get the best of you; you are strong enough!* The self-talk worked as a temporary fix, but I couldn't shake the agony in my heart. When I was alone, I cried, screamed, hit walls, and threw things, but there was no release from the misery. I could only sleep when I was so exhausted that my body just stopped. When loved ones reached out and expressed concern, I would shut them down. I made it almost impossible to be close to me. You know the "fight or flight" mode? I felt like I had taken up permanent residence there. Loud noises made me jump, and my heart was always beating too fast. My clothes were hanging on my thin frame, and I remember making myself eat just so I wouldn't keep losing weight. People were noticing how thin I was, and I did not want that kind of attention. I didn't want any attention; I just wanted to be left alone.

A little about me; I was born on June 4, 1963, the youngest of five children. We grew up in the Bay Area, in Castro Valley, California. Mom was from Texas, and as a young girl, she dreamt of moving to the big city, getting married, and raising five kids, and she did exactly that. My dad was from San Francisco, California. He would become a decorated World War II veteran and earned his doctorate in education. They were married for almost sixty years, and while they endured much suffering, including the loss of one of my brothers, they were kind and loving parents.

With five kids in our family and four cousins that lived close by, I was always surrounded by family, and I was born with a best friend, my sister, Martha, who is just a few years older than me.

I had a somewhat unpredictable home life. My parents were good providers, and we never went without, but they didn't show up for events in my life; it just didn't happen. Maybe it was that they were older and I was the last of five children; I think they were just tired. My mom was forty-two when I was born.

My parents were amazing, and we had a beautiful relationship as I grew into an adult with a family of my own. My favorite childhood memories are of me, with my siblings and cousins playing outside until dark when we would run in, scarf down our food, and ask to be excused so we could keep playing. We put on plays for every holiday, had sleepovers on weekends, and rode our bikes endlessly. We played tag, "quicksand" in the gravel pit, and we had birds, fish, dogs, cats, and rabbits that lived in our playhouse. The rabbits multiplied, and eventually there were dozens of bunnies running around our yard and in front of our house. We had apple trees, walnut trees, and a big maple tree that we climbed in. It was a good childhood; we were loved and happy.

Mom stayed at home to raise us, and our dad was a teacher, so summers meant vacations in the family station wagon. We would travel to Texas, stopping at hotels along the way, eating burgers and ice cream, fighting in the car with five of us constantly asking, "Are we there yet?" It was amazing. I remember my dad's left arm being super tan because he would always have it resting outside of the driver's side window as we drove miles and miles across the states to visit family in Texas.

When my oldest brother packed his bags, loaded his green Pinto with his belongings, and left for Northwestern University, the drinking started, or at least I started to notice it. I was around twelve. Overall, I feel like I had a good childhood, but my parent's drinking really bothered me and seemed to affect every part of my life. I ached for the day I could make my own money, move out, and become independent, living life on my terms. I needed order and structure. I craved discipline and rules because I never had them. Looking back, I realize that I desperately wanted to live an orderly life and sought control in everything. I moved out at sixteen, and while I made some stupid choices, I was always responsible. I wasn't afraid of hard work and took as many jobs as I needed to make ends meet.

I couldn't wait to get out of town; I had gone to school with the same kids from kindergarten through my senior year in high school, and I was bored. I always felt like I was a little bit different than others and was more comfortable with people older than me, which worked out since I was the youngest in the family. My sister's and brother's friends welcomed me, and I mostly hung out with them. I had my own set of friends that I was close to, but as soon as we entered high school we drifted apart, and I was fine with that.

I've always liked order and viewed life as black and white; right vs. wrong; fair and unfair. I'm typically decisive and hold strong opinions. My mom wrote a poem for me when I was eighteen, and one line reads so true "about Kathryn Mae there is a lot to be known, she is up or she is down, there is no in-between." That was me; extreme, intense, all in or not at all. I proceed in life by bulldozing my way through it or totally checking out. My circle was small, and I was fiercely protective of those I loved. All these characteristics were magnified when I had children of my own.

I have a heavy gait; my family and others often ask me why I walk so hard, like I'm on a mission, and I don't have an answer for that other than most of the time I do feel like I'm on a mission.

Looking back, I can honestly say that I gave my children everything I could give them, putting them first in most every aspect of life. I worked full-time and grabbed side work when I could. I showed up for school activities and sporting events. I made their lunches, brought Gatorade® to games, made favorite dinners, special birthday cakes, and homemade chocolate chip cookies for the classroom. I made sure they had a clean, safe, warm, and happy place to call home.

After the divorce from their father, I dated a little, and then I met Darwin. We dated for about fifteen years and then moved in together for a year before we finally got married. People wondered why we waited so long, and there were a lot of reasons, but mostly, for me, I didn't want to add any more stress to our lives. I wanted to raise my boys and focus on them before I did anything else. The divorce was hard, and I felt like they needed all of me; I didn't want to divide my attention. Darwin and I made it work, and our kids grew up loving each other, and to this day they are all close.

Raising the boys was a joy. Holidays were filled with fun surprises and traditions. Our rule was that no one was allowed to leave their bedroom to peek under the Christmas tree until everyone was up and ready. Every single time, Justin and I woke up first, and we would end up jumping on Dillon's bed, trying to wake him so Christmas could begin. Dillon would always take his time, appearing uninterested just to make Justin crazy. It was fun and exciting. I had a strict budget, so birthdays and holidays were my time for special gifts; one from me, some from Santa, one from our dog Maggie, one from Mrs. Claus, and one from a reindeer or two. The stockings were always overflowing with treats including an orange, banana, socks, Chapstick, and our favorite rice candy.

I tried my best to give them what they needed including boundaries, rules, love, and affection. I taught them how to shake hands, to have a good work ethic, and how important it is to keep your word. They were taught to be gentlemen, open doors, make their bed, carry groceries, respect their elders, say please and thank you, and always be kind. We had values and manners; we were intense and a bit high strung, but we were happy. Our home was always humming with loud music and laughter.

I never could afford out-of-state trips, but every summer we planned a beach trip with our friends, the Fahey's. Kathy and Dennis Fahey are like family, and their sons are the same ages as my boys. Cody and Justin met in kindergarten, and Dillon and Ryan met right after that; they grew up together and became lifelong friends. Every year Kathy and I would pack up our boys and head to Santa Cruz or Monterey. These were always fun times that left us with beautiful memories.

I remember one trip to the beach in Santa Cruz on an overcast day. The sun would peek out from behind the clouds from time to time, but it was chilly. Justin was neck deep in the ocean and came running in for a snack. I asked him if he was cold and wanted a towel. He looked at me with his lips turning blue and teeth chattering so badly he could barely get the words out, and replied, "No Mom, I'm fine, I'm not even cold, I'm going back in!" and off he ran, plunging back into the freezing cold ocean. Justin always pushed things to the limit and lived for each new adventure.

Their father took them to Disneyland, fishing, and camping trips, and his parents, their Nana and Papa, were active in their lives as well. They always attended their ball games, took them camping, and showered them with love. Aunt Martha and Uncle Ed took the boys on a fabulous annual vacation to Disney World, Hawaii, the circus, and many other fun places. They would come home full of excitement, telling me about all the fun they had until they were too tired to talk anymore. Then they would crawl in their beds exhausted from the thrill of their latest adventure. They were happy boys, surrounded by love.

But there were hard times too. As the boys got older and entered adolescence, they became fiercely competitive. It was not unusual to see ping-pong paddles flying in the air if they thought the other was winning the game, or the Monopoly board game getting flipped over on the floor because someone was accused of cheating. Dillon found what buttons to push, and Justin would always react. They relentlessly got under each other's skin, and yet, would protect each other in any circumstance that involved others. I still don't understand why they fought so much, but they did, and not just with each other. There were countless broken noses, bloody ears, and swollen knuckles, either from sports or fights. They both had explosive tempers and a hard time controlling it. I bought a punching bag for the garage and signed them up for all the sports they wanted to play so they would have an outlet for whatever might be brewing inside. They loved sports; the more aggressive and competitive, the more they liked it. I remember frequently hearing from their football coaches how hard they hit, and I knew there was underlying anger that they brought to the field. The coaches loved it, but it worried me.

I knew part of their anger stemmed from the divorce. There was constant conflict, and they seemed to find themselves in the middle of battles between their father and I. They went back and forth between two homes that had vastly different rules, beliefs, and standards. It was hard on them. There were a lot of issues with trust and communication, and it was taking a toll on the entire family.

After high school, Justin started going downhill fast. Before I knew he was using heroin, I felt like I was going crazy. Nothing about him seemed right anymore, and strange things were happening.

Here's a glimpse of what life was like:

Scenario 1: *It's summer and we're barbecuing. I go to the kitchen, open the drawer, and pull out the aluminum foil, only to find the box empty. I'm frustrated. Why can't people in this house throw out the box and let me know we're out of foil? I could have sworn I just bought a roll. Odd. I add aluminum foil to my grocery list and borrow a sheet from the neighbor so I can barbecue the vegetables. Two weeks later, I go to get the aluminum foil and find a shredded little pile left in the box. I'm confused. You know when you leave the grocery store and can't find your car and you look hopelessly around the parking lot? I'm that kind of confused.*

Scenario 2: *The slow-cook chili is ready, and the house smells amazing. I'm setting the table with my favorite bowls and dishes. I've always told my family that presentation is everything, even when you're having a simple family dinner. The table is loaded with cornbread, chili, grated cheese to sprinkle on top, a bottle of Tapatio® for the boys, cucumber salad, and ice water with lemon. Everything is ready. I go to my silverware drawer to get the utensils and there are only two spoons. I check the dishwasher, and there are only two in there, which means we have four spoons. I count the spoons again. There should be a dozen! Where in the world are my spoons? Odd. I add spoons to my Target shopping list and tell my family to just use forks for tonight.*

Scenario 3: *My house is clean. I love the smell of bleach and Pine Sol® and an orderly house; for me it's like the best thing ever. After spending my entire Saturday cleaning, I take a quick shower, put on some comfy clothes, and settle in with a good book. The boys are home doing their thing, and suddenly there is a strange chemical smell. I put my book down and go investigate. No one knows what it is. Justin is taking a shower; I put my ear to the door of the bathroom and hear the water running. Dillon is in the kitchen warming up food. Hmm, it must be outside. I go outside and breathe in...*

nothing. I go back into the house and still smell it; it's an odd and assaulting kind of smell that overpowers the clean scent of Pine- Sol®. After about an hour, the smell dissipates, but I keep smelling it periodically in the weeks and months ahead. I find myself wondering if there is something dead under the house or in the vents that keeps filling my house with that sickening smell that I've grown to despise.

Scenario 4: *My car is always clean; I like it that way. One evening as I'm leaving work, I notice I'm on empty and head to the gas station to fill up my tank. It's dark, and I can't see where my debit card is, so I turn on the overhead lights. As I'm looking through my purse, I notice black smudges on my wallet. What the heck? I look at my fingers and see black on my fingertips. Where did that come from? I wipe my hands on a towel, fill my tank with gas, and head home. The next morning, I hop in the car and notice black smudges around the overhead light. I touch the smudge and smell my hand; I have no idea what this is. I ask the boys if they made the mess in my car, and they both say no. I notice black smudges in the bathroom and on the doorknobs. What is going on?*

Scenario 5: *I think everyone has a place to throw their spare change, right? Mine was a clear vase inside my closet. When I had spare change in my pocket or my coin purse was full, I would throw the change in the vase with the plan of doing something special when the vase was full. It was fun and felt like free money. I waited until it was full of change and then I'd take it to the grocery store coin machine and get super excited when they would cash me out in dollar bills. I would usually end up using the money for food, but always thought it would be fun to save enough change for a surprise vacation with the boys. One morning, as I'm getting my clothes out of my closet, I notice the change vase looks low. I ask the boys if they took any change, and they both deny it.*

I'm thinking it must be my mistake, but I remind them it is MY money, and they are not entitled to it; they must always ask me first. I'm irritated because I know there was more change in there but, I realize the boys have a lot of friends over. I need to be more careful about shutting my door; you never know what people will do. A month later, I notice all the silver is gone; only pennies remain. Where is my change?

Scenario 6: *I needed some ingredients for the pancakes I was planning on making in the morning, so I go to the store. I throw microwave popcorn and a box of milk duds in my cart in case Justin feels like watching a movie with me. At Safeway, in the express checkout, the cashier rings me up. The charge is $22.35. I'm grateful I got some cash earlier that week because my debit card was being replaced. I open my wallet and instead of two twenty-dollar bills, I only see one. I search my wallet and purse because I know I had two twenties. The line is forming behind me, and I'm flustered. I explain to the cashier that I'll have to write a check because I don't have enough cash, and I don't have my debit card. I can feel the irritation from the people behind me because, we are in the "express line," and I'm holding things up. I'm obsessing over the missing twenty-dollar bill.*

After about a year of questioning my own sanity, I would finally learn the truth about what was really happening with Justin. In the chapters that follow, you'll learn how things unraveled for us, but let me first explain the scenarios. Justin started by smoking heroin. He was taking the aluminum foil to hold the heroin in as he used a lighter under the foil until it created smoke, and then he would inhale it. The black smudges in my house and car were the residue the lighter left from burning the underside of the foil to smoke the dope, and the rancid, bitter smell in our house was the heroin cooking. Then he started injecting it. The spoons he took were used as a bowl to heat the heroin into liquid form so he could shoot it. My debit card was getting replaced because I thought someone was using my account number; turns out Justin was using it to take money out of my ATM

47

and would slip my card back into my wallet before I even knew it was missing, and, well, we all know where the twenty-dollar bills were going. The bills were going to the same place my change was going; to pay for Justin's drugs.

Before I knew it was heroin, all those times I was counting spoons, all those missing twenty-dollar bills, all those small things happening just got shrugged off as strange, but the entire time it was Justin in his addiction, manipulating and stealing from me so he could get high. As the truth started to surface, I found it hard to even look at my son. The lies were endless and seemed easy for him. The depths of his deception and manipulation made the deep ocean seem like shallow water. As I looked at my son, I found myself wondering who this evil person was.

My mind would flash back to the sweet, affectionate little boy that would giggle and run to me with his arms spread wide in anticipation of a big hug. The little boy that would turn his head into my neck and wrap his arms around me, appearing to revel in my love. The little boy that would yell, "Watch meeeeee!" from the backyard, wanting to show me how fast he could run through the sprinkler over, and over, and over again. The sweet little boy that somehow turned into this monster that stood before me. The reality of what we were dealing with was just too much to take in. I was shaken to my core.

"YOU WERE MADE BY GOD
AND FOR GOD AND UNTIL YOU
UNDERSTAND THAT, LIFE
WILL NEVER MAKE SENSE."

Rick Warren

Counting Spoons

KRYPTONITE

CHAPTER
THREE

JUSTIN

I was twelve years old the first time I tried alcohol. I was with my brother and some friends, and we managed to get some beer and black and mild cigarillos. I guzzled four Budweiser beers that night; it was my dad's favorite beer, so I felt like a man drinking it. We drank, smoked, and had a blast. I was staying at my dad's house at the time, and when he got home, he found me throwing up in the bathroom, and I got in trouble. Despite the sickness and punishment, I enjoyed myself and couldn't wait to do it again.

By age thirteen, I was chewing tobacco regularly. The first time my brother gave me some, it was the Skull Peach brand. Dillon laughed and made me run around in the front yard after I put it in my mouth. I remember falling down from the dizziness, but I liked it and kept chewing; I thought the buzz was amazing.

At fourteen, I tried marijuana. I was in a tree fort in the backyard at a friend's house. We bought a joint from a buddy, lit it up, and smoked the entire thing. We waited and waited and were disappointed because we didn't feel anything. Ten minutes later we were completely stoned. We stayed in that tree fort and laughed for hours.

By fifteen, I was drinking on weekends with friends and having a good time. I remember going to a concert with a buddy; his mom bought us a bunch of beer and liquor to drink on the way. My mom would have flipped out if she knew my friend's mom bought it for us, but she never found out. We always seemed to find a way to get alcohol.

By sixteen, I had tried Ecstasy/Molly's (hallucinogenic), Concerta (stimulant), and Tramadol (pain killer), Shrooms (hallucinogenic), and Vicodin (pain killer). It wasn't just me; most of my friends were doing it too. At seventeen, I was popping Vicodin and snorting Oxycontin, and that was an entirely different kind of high. Up until this point, nothing had gripped me. Not alcohol, weed, or ecstasy, but the opiates gave me a warm feeling and I immediately started to chase it. At this point, I was still performing athletically and doing okay academically. I was working out daily, and I looked like a healthy teenager. It wasn't until I got expelled from school that things really started to unravel.

All my talents and confidence seemed to heighten if I was buzzed. I was the starting quarterback on the football team and the catcher for the baseball team. I drove a white, 1991 Chevy Z71 Extended Cab. I was friends with the campus supervisor, so I had the freedom to come and go as I pleased. I had a tight group of friends, and we were wild. I felt like I always took things a little farther than others and would do just about anything to have a good time. It was all about partying and having fun for me. I had lots of friends, but I had enemies as well. You either loved me or hated me, and I thrived on both. The more I used drugs, the more fights I got into, and the partying started to get out of control. I began my spiral without even knowing what hit me.

It's my senior year, football season is fast approaching, and I get a text from my good friend, Van. He asked me to come by his house after practice. I pull into his driveway just in time to see him being wheeled out on a stretcher by a paramedic. Van put a gun in his mouth and blew his brains out that day. My larger than life, God-loving, fearless, beautiful friend killed himself. I will never know why he took his own life or why he texted me that day. My heart is shattered, but I keep numbing myself and carry on.

It's the day before homecoming, and I'm getting ready for the most exciting game I'd ever play in, and I get busted. I went to the parking lot to grab a chew out of my truck during lunch, which is against school policy. A new campus supervisor saw me and decided to search my truck. After about thirty minutes they found something they could use to get rid of me; my dad's old fishing knife with a 3-inch blade. They called it a weapon and expelled me. My world and self-worth ended. My dreams of playing college ball slipped right through my hands. I was alone. I was not on a team. I was a failure. I was lost, and I had no idea what to do. It was like hitting a brick wall and falling into a big, black, endless hole.

Up until this point, I had figured out how to get the attention I wanted. Sports, girls, friends, and fights made me feel important. It was my identity and now it was gone. I didn't know what to do, and I didn't have the tools to deal with failure or rejection, so I crashed. I crashed hard. I'd been practicing feeling better and numbing myself on drugs and alcohol for a while, so that's where I turned for comfort. I had to numb myself, so I didn't feel like such a failure.

I still needed to graduate, so I tried going to two different schools in the area. The first school ended in just two days because a couple of defensive linemen shoulder bumped me, and fists started flying. I would not put up with anything. We went at it in the hallway, and I got kicked out right away. It seemed like fighting, popping pills, and chasing girls fueled me.

The second school lasted a few months. It was a private Christian school. I was excited because two of my best friends went there, and I started dating a girl that I really liked. What they didn't like was my "bad boy" attitude, and before I knew it, I had made quite a few enemies. I couldn't deal with the preppy Christian girl attitudes, and I couldn't take the gossip and drama, and people didn't like that I was selling weed. At least the non-stoners didn't like it.

I was out of options, so I finished high school on independent study and somehow was able to keep it together long enough to graduate. By this time, I was using heavy. The fights continued, but they were different. I wasn't fighting in self-defense or to protect someone else; I was fighting because I was angry, and I wanted to hurt someone. I was isolated, depressed, and withdrawn, and my only pleasure was getting high, and that's what I did. I got high every day using whatever I could find, until one evening, a buddy and I did heroin together. That's when I found my kryptonite. When I smoked it, I melted into the seat in my truck, and my entire body floated. All the pain went away, and nothing seemed to matter anymore; I didn't care about anything. The next morning it was all I could think about.

It wasn't long until my family noticed my weight loss, paling skin, and that things were missing around the house. I was wearing sweats and it was ninety degrees outside. I was a disaster. As my addiction worsened, so did my relationships with everyone I loved. My world just kept getting smaller and smaller, and then everything spiraled out of control.

"THERE WILL STILL BE DAYS
WHEN THERE ARE
MOUNTAINS AND VALLEYS
AHEAD OF YOU, BUT YOU
WILL LEARN AND GROW FROM
ALL OF THEM."

Morgan Harper Nichols

HE DROPPED OFF

CHAPTER

FOUR

KATHRYN 2011

It was a particularly long day at work, and I'm relieved to finally be home. Both the boys are out, so I have a little time to unwind. I start making dinner because I know Dillon's going to call me on the way home from his workout wanting to know what we're eating. I light the barbecue and get the tri-tip and chicken out of the marinade and onto the grill. I make a big green salad, slice the French bread, and put the butter out to soften. The asparagus is steaming, the lemon wedges are cut, and within an hour, dinner is ready.

It's still early, and the boys won't be home for a while. I'm hungry, so I slice off some of the chicken, take a good portion of the asparagus, and put it in a bowl to eat while I'm standing in the kitchen deciding what to do next.

I eat and feel better; the lingering headache of the day is fading and I'm relieved. I cover the food and put it away until the boys get home. Happy to have that accomplished, I wash my dishes, straighten the house, pour myself a glass of red wine, take a seat on the couch and slowly exhale.

It isn't long before Dillon is home and taking dinner back out of the refrigerator to warm up. He piles massive amounts of food on his plate and digs in. He's pure muscle; not an ounce of fat on his 5'11" frame, and he eats every meal as if there won't be a next one. I feel like I'm always cooking for and cleaning up after these boys, and I wouldn't change it even if I could. Each meal is eagerly devoured with words of appreciation; they always thank me, and I love that.

As Dillon eats, we chat about our day, and he seems to have had a good one, which lifts my mood. He finishes his meal, and I see him look at the table. He's looking at the food that needs to be put away, the table that needs to be wiped off, and his stack of dirty dishes. He pauses for just a moment before he looks at me and says, "Any chance you can take care of all this, or do I need to?" his hand motioning in circles above the kitchen table. I glare at him pretending to be mad, and he flashes his best smile and, after a few seconds of considering his request, I wave him off and tell him he owes me big time. He jumps to the ground and throws himself up in an impressive handstand and knocks out twenty push-ups in celebration of dodging cleaning duties. He grabs me for a quick hug of gratitude, lets out a full belly burp, and heads down the hall to shower. I smile as I'm cleaning up after him.

We watch a little TV together, and then Dillon asks where his brother is. I tell him I'm not sure and have been asking myself the same thing for the last thirty minutes. It's dark and late on a Tuesday night, and he should be home by now. Dillon assures me that Justin will be home soon and says he's probably still at their dad's house. He heads to his room shouting a "goodnight" over his shoulder. He's eager to get his eight hours of sleep before conditioning with his baseball coach at 7:00 a.m. sharp. I wish I could go to bed too, because I am so over this day, but instead I wait up for Justin.

Around 10:30 p.m. I hear the door. It's him. He says he's fine, and he's sorry for not calling; he was with his dad. Justin darts into his room, and I follow noticing that he won't make eye contact with me. He shuts his door, and I start to open it when he puts his hand on it to stop me.

"Mom, can you just give me a minute?"

I stop and back off. With the door between us, I ask if he's hungry. He says he ate at his dads but would love a milkshake. I hate that he doesn't eat tonight because he looks thin to me. I tell him to get ready for bed, and that I'll go get him a milkshake. "I'll be right back, Son."

I stop at the gas station to put gas in my car in order to save time in the morning, because I'm already stressing about not getting enough sleep tonight. I hate feeling anxious, but I do. It feels like a storm is brewing, and I don't know what direction it's coming from.

I come back and knock on his door to give him the extra-large Oreo milkshake with whipped cream that he requested. He opens the door just enough to get the shake and immediately closes it.

"Thanks Mom, I'm exhausted, so goodnight." I stand at his door for a few minutes and debate on going in to talk to him. It's late, and I'm exhausted, so I decide against it and go to my room, carrying my racing thoughts with me. He doesn't look good, and he's acting strange. I think about Dillon this evening and wonder when the last time was that I saw Justin workout. His once healthy, muscular body now looks frail.

I have two sons who just a few months ago were on the same path. Healthy, strong, competitive, energetic, young men, hungry for whatever life had to offer, and then suddenly Justin dropped off.

I lie in my bed for about an hour, and sleep doesn't come, so I get up and check on them as I often do. Dillon and our Labrador mix, Maggie, the rescue we've had for over twelve years, are both sound asleep, snoring softly. I move on to Justin's door and slowly open it, uneasy about what I might find. His TV is blaring, he's sitting up holding his milkshake, but he has nodded off. His head drooping to the side, the milkshake spilling over onto his bed. I stand there in the doorway and stare at him.

My mind drifts back to the many other nights I've checked on the boys. Dillon has always been easy; he loved sleep and was proudly independent. He would get his blanket, say goodnight, and wake up nine hours later, but Justin was much different. He fought sleep and seemed disappointed that the day had to end. After a drink of water and a few "goodnights," he would give in and then usually show up in my room asking if he could snuggle with me for a little while before he went back to his own bed like a "big boy." I'd usually say yes, and he would drift off to sleep, snuggled up with his arms and legs stretched out and tangled in the blankets. Later in the night I would pick up the little boy that was growing like a weed and take him back to his bed.

I shake the memory and feel burdened by this night and the

sight of Justin lying in his bed with the light of the TV shining on his skin that looks so pale. Something is very wrong. I take the milkshake, throw a towel over the mess, turn off the TV and close his door, wondering what has happened to my sweet little boy.

JUSTIN

My stomach is turning, and I'm sweating. I need to get high. I was hoping Dillon and Mom were asleep, but the lights are on, and I'm guessing Mom is awake and waiting up for me. I hate when she does that. I feel like she's always looking me over, trying to figure out what's wrong. I want to scream at her, "Drugs, Mom! I've turned into a drug addict!" But there's no way I'm telling her anything. I've got this. I'll handle it. I need to keep a roof over my head, and I need money—I've got to make this work.

I walk in the door and make a quick turn into my room and am relieved that she doesn't follow me. I need to be alone so I can smoke this. I lie and tell her I was at my dad's because I know she'll never call him to check. They don't talk, and they don't like each other much, so that works in my favor these days. I've gotten good at lying, and most of the time she buys it.

I've spent the last half-hour trying to make myself look good in case she interrogates me tonight. I took a shower at my buddy's house while I was waiting for our dope. I used eye drops, dabbed some cologne on, and put on a fresh white t-shirt. Before I walked in the house, I slapped my cheeks, trying to get some color back in my face. As I look in the mirror, I can see that my skin looks pale, but, it's not really that bad. I can manage this. I say this in my head about a hundred times a day.

I get to my room, and she's asking me questions, but she doesn't push too hard tonight. Bonus! She's leaving to get me a milkshake. Now I can smoke out of the window in my room without dealing with her. I set it up, light it, and breathe it in. I feel the black smoke fill my lungs. There it is, the soothing warmness that slowly, perfectly, saturates my body. My heart rate slows, my stomach settles down, my sweats stop, and just like that, everything is good again.

I hurry and check her room before she gets home just in case she left some cash on her dresser, or change in her closet. She used to do that a lot but hasn't lately. I wonder what she thinks is happening to it. Every time I take something from her, I promise myself it's going to be the last time, but it's just so easy. I feel like it's sitting there beckoning me to take it. I'll make it up to her at some point when I decide to get clean, but I'm not ready yet. Every time I've tried to stop using, my entire body hurts, and I can't handle that right now; not just yet.

Every day, it's the same thing; I have to figure out how to get money so I can get more drugs. There's something about the pursuit that excites me. Just knowing that sweet black smoke will get me high keeps me going.

I'm feeling good now, but I have to be ready for when mom gets home. I spray air freshener, just in case she decides to come in my room and have another talk. She doesn't ever stop; I get so tired of trying to keep her calm. I wish she would just leave me alone to do my thing.

The rumble of the garage door catches me by surprise—Mom's back home already. She's going to walk in the house any second so I rush back into my room and prop one foot against the door, blocking it—she cannot find out I'm smoking dope! As her footsteps get close, I crack the door open just enough to take the milkshake, then quickly close it again. "Thanks Mom, I'm exhausted. Goodnight." I lean my whole body against the door waiting to see what she's gonna do. *PLEASE just go to bed!* Within minutes the hallway light goes out, and then all is quiet. Relief spreads throughout my entire body as I flip off the lights, turn on the TV, peel off my clothes, and melt into my bed. The whipped cream tastes sweet on my tongue as the milkshake floats down my throat and quenches my thirst. The dark waves swirl around, pulling me under, and call me into oblivion.

Counting Spoons

NOT READY FOR THE TRUTH

CHAPTER
FIVE

KATHRYN

Dillon was in college playing baseball and would come home during the off season to train and work, trying to earn enough money to get through the next baseball season. I always felt relief when Dillon was home. Not just because he was strong and supportive, but because we had developed a special friendship, and I enjoyed his company. Having him home made me feel safe and protected. I trusted him implicitly.

I was proud of all that Dillon had accomplished and how hard he worked. He had one goal, and that was to play baseball. It was fun for me when he was home because the routine was the same. Eat, train, eat, work, eat, train, eat, sleep and repeat. He didn't let anyone, or anything get in the way of his goals.

I remember him coming home for spring break when Justin was deep in his addiction. Justin had borrowed Dillon's friend's jeans and came home late that evening smelling like smoke. He reeked badly when he walked in and was obviously high, or drunk, or on something. I was sitting in the living room watching Dillon and his friend Blake, watch Justin.

Have you ever done that? Watched someone watch someone else to try and get a glimpse of what they might be seeing or thinking?

Searching their eyes, trying to see what they see? I do it all the time. Like a beautiful baby being held by her aunt who is meeting her for the first time; you watch the love in auntie's eyes as she takes in the beauty of her perfect little niece; the love so strong that it's showing all over her face. Or when your child makes a mistake, and you watch your husband as he talks to your scared little 9-year-old son, hoping to see compassion in his eyes as he decides what his punishment will be. When you meet your son's girlfriend for the first time, and you watch how she looks at him, and him at her, and you wonder if she might be "the one." Or when someone you love is acting like a stranger, and you search the eyes of others, wondering if they're seeing the same ugliness that you see.

Back to that evening, as I'm watching this transpire in front of me, I'm mortified and embarrassed. I get on Justin's case for borrowing the pants without permission, for smelling like smoke, for being high, and for just, well, for everything. I look at Dillon and Blake as they sit in silence. I listen to Justin apologize and make excuses and try to act cool, and it makes my stomach turn; I just want to disappear.

The next day, when Dillon and I were alone, I mentioned the night before and said it made Justin look bad. Dillon was leaning over our dining room chair lacing up his baseball cleats when he stopped, looked up at me, and with as much gentleness as I'm sure he could muster, he said, "That's because he *is* really bad, Mom."

I felt like I got punched in the stomach. I knew Justin was bad. I didn't know exactly what was going on, but I knew it was bad. Deep inside, I felt like we were losing him, but to hear Dillon declare it out loud somehow made it real. He was being honest, but I wasn't quite ready for the truth. I wanted Dillon to tell me it's not that bad. I wanted him to say that I'm overreacting, to tell me everything will be alright or not to worry. Justin will be fine. But he didn't say any of those things. Dillon was the levelheaded, strong, rational one in the house, and he didn't get rattled easily. Growing up, he had to deal with me and Justin—two people who were much more intense and reactive, and I know that had to be hard on him. To hear my logical, levelheaded Dillon, my beloved oldest son, say that his brother was in trouble gutted me. I think he sensed my reaction to his words because he walked over and hugged me. Dillon did not express his feelings often, but he said a lot with his hugs. They were strong and protective. He held on a bit longer than usual and then asked if I was going to be alright. I assured him I was fine. He said he was headed to the batting cages and asked if I needed anything before he left. I smiled and said no.

I heard the front door shut then the sound of Dillon's car trunk pop open, the thud of his gear dropping, the slam of the trunk, tapping of his cleats, the engine humming, his car door shutting, and then I heard him drive away. I heard the small, white clock ticking as it sat on the shelf in the living room where I was sitting. I heard kids playing outside and Maggie yawn as she stretched out on her bed next to the couch, and I just sat there. I sat right there in the same spot until after dark; I couldn't seem to move. I sat there motionless, empty, staring at nothing, not thinking of anything, just sitting there, frozen in fear.

JUSTIN

I wake up to the sound of dishes banging around in the kitchen and cover my face with my pillow. I feel miserable. My mouth is dry, my head hurts, and my body aches. I shake my head, sit up, and close one eye, squinting so I can make out the time on the wall clock. It's 10:30 a.m. I try to think. Why is Mom home doing dishes instead of at work? I realize it's Saturday. That sucks because she'll be here all weekend. I can't find my phone. It's a piece of crap. I sold the nice iPhone Mom got me, so I'm using one of the old phones we had lying around. She thinks I lost it and that's what I want her to think.

I sit up and look at the jeans on the floor and remember last night. I had been up for two days on meth and was tripping hard. I knew I was coming home, so I drank as much vodka as I could to come down. I was hoping for an empty house, but Dillon, Blake, and Mom were all in the living room with every light in the house on; I felt like I was walking into a spotlight. I wonder if they could tell I was high. I did my best to act normal, but I'm not sure if I pulled it off. Mom was mad, but Dillon and Blake seemed fine.

I take a deep breath and start to plan this day, trying to figure out how I'm going to get my hands on some money. This keeps getting harder and harder, but I've got to get some soon, or I'm going to feel really sick in the next few hours.

I hear footsteps, loud ones, and I know it's my mom. I lay back down and cover my head and pretend to be asleep. I hear my door open.

"Justin, you need to wake up, and we need to talk. . . . Son, wake up." I stay under the covers hoping she'll go away and leave me alone.

"Justin!"

She pulls my sheets back.

"Mom! What the heck? I'm trying to sleep, leave me alone!" I pull the covers back over my head, eyes closed, willing her to please just go away!

"We need to talk about last night! What is your problem, Son? What is going on? You reeked of smoke and borrowed Blake's pants without asking! What were you thinking? You look terrible, and you're acting strange; you need to tell me what is going on!"

I stay under the covers and respond.

"OK, Mom! Just let me sleep for another hour and then we can talk. I'm fine, why do you always exaggerate everything? Just let me sleep, I have a headache." I hear her take a deep breath and slam my door as hard as she can which isn't hard because I've punched so many holes in it that it doesn't close right anymore. She's finally out of my room, and I take a minute, trying to figure this out. Hopefully, something will come up in the next hour, and she'll leave so I can take off without having to see her.

I wait and wait and finally hear the garage door. I tip-toe out of my bedroom and look out the front window. Dillon's car is gone. I look in the garage, and Mom's car is gone. Perfect. I see a note on the table.

"Justin, do not leave. I'll be home in an hour, and we need to talk. DO NOT LEAVE THIS HOUSE!"

I've got to get out of here quick, because knowing my mom, she'll be back in thirty minutes.

I don't have time for a shower, so I grab my clothes and scan the house. I grab a few pairs of her shoes out of her closet, I find one of Dillon's college sweatshirts and about fifteen quarters. I should be able to get twenty dollars at the consignment store for the clothes; I'm a regular there, and they usually give me a fair price. I should have enough for at least one bag of heroin. I can almost taste it already. I feel a wave of energy, and my heart rate jumps in anticipation. I'm ready to go. I grab a green trash bag, throw the clothes in it, and put the change in my pocket.

I close my door and go in the backyard to say goodbye to Maggie, who loves me no matter what. I look at her, rub her ears, and she responds with the thump of her wagging tail on the ground. "I love you girl, you know that, right?" She looks at me with what seems like sad eyes.

"I'm okay Mags, I've got this handled, I'll be fine." I kiss her long black nose and then take off; gotta chase that dragon.

Counting Spoons

THE SAME CLOTH

CHAPTER
SIX

DILLON

I was away in college playing baseball for most of the dark times. Baseball was my world back then, and it was an easy escape from everything that was going on with my brother. When I'd come home during holidays and the off-season, I started noticing a change in him. His eyes were shifty. He talked too much; he was trying too hard, always acting suspicious. "Can I use your car for a minute?" and "Hey, you got $20, you can spot me?" or "What are your plans tonight?" It was as if he was calculating his next move. It felt like I was meeting a stranger. There came a time when the signs couldn't be ignored, and I knew Justin was in deep, but I never imagined it was heroin.

Everything about Justin's addiction was hard, but the lies were tough to deal with. My brother lied about everything; even when it didn't seem necessary. And what added fuel to the fire was my mom questioning everything he said. He was up to no good, and Mom was not one to shy away from calling him out, but her constant need to know what was happening with Justin made everything worse. I knew he was ashamed of his secret and bringing it to his attention constantly was not helpful. On top of the lies, I watched him make one bad decision after the next, and he was doing things that didn't fit with who he was as a person. I remember him telling me he was selling weed, like he was proud of it. I jumped on his case, "Is this who you want to be, dude? What are you doing? You better be careful; this isn't a joke!" He could tell I wasn't impressed by his side hustle, or the money he hoped he would be making. I knew he was listening to me, and he cared about what I thought, but it didn't stop him.

It wrecked me to watch him act so desperate, and he looked so bad. He's always been a top athlete and physically fit, but drugs stripped him down. He was small on drugs; skinny, pale, wide-eyed. Like a ghost.

I remember coming home from college and noticing Justin taking obnoxiously long showers. There would be a rancid, brown sugar kind of smell that would seep into the house from under the door of the bathroom he was in. I knew something was going on, but I wasn't sure what it was.

Mom was wound tight. She was still going through the motions, working, exercising, and doing what she does, but she was on edge. She would prepare big spreads of food for me and my friends, but she didn't join us. When I asked her about it, she would tell me she had eaten earlier or wasn't hungry, but I know she wasn't eating much. Mom was strong, but her stress was showing. You could almost see the frenzy she was in and feel the energy bouncing off her. It was intense.

When I was on the road and called home, I could hear the tension in Mom's voice, and it left me feeling helpless. I was pissed off at Justin for what he was putting her through, and I didn't understand it. I did not think it was possible for him to change so much. We'd always been like-minded, and we had an unspoken agreement as brothers about who we are and how we live our lives, but that all went away when he was on drugs. I knew he looked up to me and that he didn't want to let me down, but it was clear that this thing had a grip on him. When he and I were home at the same time, he was always careful and avoided me as much as possible.

When Justin was in rehab, Mom tried to stay as busy as possible. I think she was trying to fill every moment so she didn't worry about how Justin was doing. Honestly, some of those times were great. I felt like she needed to cling to something, and that something was me. She wanted me to train her in fitness and teach her about nutrition and healthy eating so she could reach some of her goals. It seemed like she wanted someone to tell her what to do so she didn't have to think. I'd carve out time and we'd go to the track and do fitness circuits, and she worked hard. It was fun. Mom and I really connected during those times, not just as mother and son, but as friends. I knew she depended on me and that was fine. I was happy to be strong for her.

Back to Justin. One of the things we did as brothers was lie on the couch, each of us taking our normal spot, and we'd watch movies, or sports. It was good, kind of our brother thing. I remember one night, we were watching football together, and I saw him dozing, nodding off, and then he was out. I knew he wasn't dead, but I couldn't wake him, and it scared me. I yelled and shook him until he finally stirred and opened his eyes, but he was out of it. That's when it hit me just how bad he was. This isn't recreational, or just a bad night, this is a serious problem.

Even in the worst of it, I never had resentment for him. I could almost see Justin's shame covering him; like he was drenched in it. I knew he hated himself and that's all I could think about. I was mad and wanted to beat him with my fists, but more than that, I wanted to rescue him. Save him from all of it. You must understand, Justin is my one and only brother. We are cut from the same cloth. We're more the same than different. I was confused about what he was doing, but I wasn't judging him. I knew he took the twenty-dollar bills that were missing from my wallet, and I knew he hated himself as he was taking my flat screen TV to the pawnshop. Even when he took my favorite Chico State hooded sweatshirt, I didn't say anything. But it hurt me. It hurt badly. That hoodie represented everything I had accomplished in baseball up until that point. It's the first hoodie I cut a V into the neckline, so it fit perfectly. It's what I wore when it was cold, when I worked out, and when I went to drink coffee in the morning. It was my team's colors, and I freaking loved it. None of the other stuff really mattered to me, but my sweatshirt did. I never confronted him about it. Why would I want to make him feel worse than he already did? I was more concerned about the addiction he was fighting than the bad things he was doing. My brother was never gone; he was just lost. I'd wait for him to call me, and he would. He didn't call much, but when he did, I would listen and respond with something encouraging, one hundred percent of the time. I felt like he desperately needed something from me; to say it's going to be okay, or that he's going to get through this, and that he wouldn't always be this way. He needed to know I was still there for him, and I was. I would always be there for Justin. I knew this wasn't going to be the last of him. At this point I hadn't recognized my faith, but I never gave up hope.

I don't gossip, so I kept to myself about Justin's journey. As far as I was concerned it was no one's business. People can be crappy sometimes, and they feed off other's misery, so I wasn't going to give anyone the satisfaction of hearing about Justin being down. I would defend my brother no matter what, and I wasn't going to tolerate anyone talking bad about him. Even when he was in rehab, I didn't tell anyone about it, unless I was certain they were really concerned about his well-being. Somewhere in me I knew he would pull through and break out of this thing he was in and, in a way, I understood it. Life can be rough! And pain can be a powerful motivator. I can't imagine what kind of pain my brother had to be in to take the path he was on.

There wasn't much I could do to help Justin or my mom, so I stuck to my routine and laid low, hoping things would get better. It felt good to get to the track or batting cages and just get after it. Work out, get my heart rate up, and let the stress pour out of my body in sweat. I had one goal, and that was to get as far as I could playing baseball. I tried hard to focus on baseball and nothing else.

Having my family watch my games online when I was in Canada, New Mexico, or Maryland, or wherever I was playing, meant everything to me. I loved it. I'll never forget playing for the Mavericks in Canada. It was my first game as a newcomer from California. My first at bat I hit a jack. A solid one, way over the fence, and I sailed around those bases as the crowd cheered me on. It was a special night, and I was getting messages on my phone from friends and my parents, but not my brother, and that struck me as odd. At that point I thought everything was good at home. I did not realize my mom was so stressed, or that my dad was checked out, and I didn't know my brother was in deep trouble. It never occurred to me that our lives could take such a drastic turn.

Justin and I never really talked directly about his addiction, and

I never gave him too much grief, but I hated it. It is truly a hopeless feeling watching your flesh and blood fall into such a dark place. I couldn't figure out what to do, but I always stayed in control of my emotions. I didn't really have a choice because everyone else was falling apart.

LIES, LIES, AND MORE LIES

CHAPTER

SEVEN

KATHRYN

Have you heard the saying, "An alcoholic will lie and say they didn't steal your wallet, but an addict will help you look for the wallet they stole from you?" It's true. The deception and lying are beyond comprehension.

For instance, my son calling from his work in San Jose (81 miles away) saying he needed forty dollars in his account to cover auto parts for his boss. I think about it; I'm angry, but I'm also busy at work and don't want to deal with him. I quickly transfer the forty dollars into his account from my account through online banking, only to discover he took the forty dollars out of the ATM that was down the street from me, literally five minutes away.

One night I'm lying in bed wide awake, with the lights out and my purse on the floor next to me. I hear something and freeze. I see Justin crawling in my room on his hands and knees trying to get to my purse without waking me. I scream at him and turn on the light; he stands, looking shocked and offended.

"Mom, don't you understand? It's just a game I was playing to see if you would wake up!" The memory of that night still haunts me.

The lies are endless and even unnecessary at times. All the stories, the chaos, the lost phones, getting jumped in a fight, bikes stolen, police detained him for no reason, lost wallet, lost friends, lost minds, loss, loss, loss, everything lost in the dark, miserable despair of addiction. The mind is a crazy thing. Even at their best, an addict is trying to manipulate anyone in any way to get more drugs. On the way to rehab, after completing detox, on the way to a family reunion, on Christmas morning, there is only one thing on their mind—and that is to get more dope. They will lie to anyone, steal from everyone, put innocent people in harm's way, and bring danger to the life of people they love.

You've heard stories of mothers selling their children in prostitution, dads selling their baby's formula and diapers for dope? I believe all of it. Addicts justify everything in their mind to get that next high. And when they come down from the drugs, when the high wears off, and the guilt and shame come creeping in, they can't take it. The reality of what they've done and who they've become is too much, so they numb themselves again. The battle continues, and the cycle of self-destruction slowly eats away at them until they are left hollow and broken. Nothing but dark, lonely, brokenness.

JUSTIN

I'm freaking out. I have to get money. I make sure no one is home before I sneak into the house. I lost my key, so I have to crawl through the bathroom window. I take a quick glance in the mirror and don't recognize myself. Do I look that different? Is it really that bad? I wash my face and try to fix my hair, so it covers my pale forehead. I look down at the sweats that are hanging on my hip bones. Whatever, I don't really care. When I get clean, I'll start lifting again, and I'll get back in shape in no time.

I have to hurry because I can't see Mom right now. I don't have the strength or patience to handle her questions. I hate the way she looks at me; I feel like she's staring into my soul. She knows I'm using, but she doesn't have any idea what or how much. I see the drug test kits on the counter in the bathroom and make a mental note to get someone to piss for me before I come back home tonight. I cannot get kicked out of this house.

I search each room, desperately trying to find something that will put money in my hands. I am going to meet my dealer in two hours, and I'm wondering how I'll make it that long because I'm getting sicker and sicker by the minute. I scan Mom's closet. She's noticing things are missing, so I have to be careful. I take a pair of shoes that are in the back and hope she doesn't look for them any time soon. I think I can get at least $10 for them at the consignment store.

I rummage through her bathroom and pick up a gold ring I find in her jewelry box. I put it back down and stare at it. I think this ring means something to her. I pick it back up and put it in my pocket. I'll pawn it and then buy it back before she even notices it's gone.

I look around the house wondering what else I can take, and then I hear the front door. I run quickly out the back and take off down the alley.

I wonder if Grandma is home. I walk over to her place and test the door. It's open and she's not here. My heart rate increases. I check the top drawer in the dresser in her closet, and there's two twenty-dollar bills. Now I can feel my heart beat all the way to my temples. She's always told me if I needed anything to just ask, and I know if she was here, she would say yes. I take one of the twenties. It's not really stealing if it's from your family, right? Grandma loves me and wouldn't want me to be sick. I squeeze my eyes shut, take a deep breath, and take the other twenty. I will put it back after I make some money doing side jobs. I run out and shut the door behind me, praying no one ever finds out.

I feel like death, and my anxiety is screaming inside of me. I'm drenched in sweat, and I haven't showered in days. I just have to get to my dealer, and then everything will be okay. I barely make it in time, but I make it. I hand him my cash, and he gives me a bag. I set up right there because I can't wait one more minute. I use more than I normally would because I'm sick, and I *need* more.

The warmth starts in my stomach and then floods to every part of my body. My muscles loosen, and my heart rate slows. I can barely keep my eyes open. I drop to my knees and lean back against the cement wall and try to count the rocks on the ground by my shoes. One, two, three, four....

I feel the buzz of my phone in my pants pocket, and it wakes me.

I see the rocks by my feet and look up; the sun is setting and it's starting to get dark. I wonder how long I've been here. I sit up, look at my phone, and see I have five missed calls from my mom. That's not good. I rub my face and feel grateful that I'm not sick but wonder how many hours I have until I feel bad again. I wish I hadn't used so much; man, I wish I would have saved some.

I think about the things I stole to get high and quickly shift my thoughts. I can't worry about that now; I'll make it right with them. At some point when this is all over, they will understand why I had to do these things. No one could manage this kind of sickness. It's time to start weaning off. I think I'll start using less. I'll save some each time, so I use less and less every day until I'm healthy again. I have to get a handle on this.

I reach in my pocket and feel Mom's ring that I still have to pawn. That should give me enough money so I can get dope to get through the night. I drop my phone back in my pocket only to hear it buzz again. I wish she would just stop!

I pawn the ring and get forty dollars for it. Awesome! I go to my buddy's house and wait for the dope. I've got to pull myself together before I go back home. I have to go, or I'm going to be on the street. Mom's getting less and less patient with me, and she doesn't seem worried anymore; she just seems mad. I feel like she hates me.

I take a hot shower, hoping the water will sting my skin and put some color back in my face. I lean my head against the tile and let the water run over me. As I look at my body, I notice how small my arms are; they used to be big and muscular. My skin feels thin somehow. I watch the dirty water circle the drain and trickle down. I use the soap to scrub away the filth, and feel like crying. I close my eyes and try to think of something to look forward to. There's a knock on the door. The dealer is here. That's what I've got to look forward to; that's all that matters right now. I shut off the water, dry myself off, put on the same dirty sweats and head out.

I start rehearsing in my head, "Hi Mom, sorry I didn't call you, but my phone died again. I was at dad's house. I got a side job working on his friend's car, so I'll be able to pay you back some of what I owe you. I met a girl and I'm taking her to get ice cream this weekend. I know I'm pale. I got the stomach flu, but I'm starting to feel better." That should be enough to distract her. I remember the drug test and forgot to get someone to piss for me. I'll just tell her I can't pee; probably because I was so sick when I was at dad's and I'm dehydrated. I can almost see her walking to the refrigerator to get me a Gatorade. Okay, I'm ready. I walk up to the house; the lights are on, and I can hear the TV. Here goes nothin...

AN EERIE FEELING

CHAPTER
EIGHT

KATHRYN JULY 2012

For the last five years, Darwin has gone on an annual six-day fishing trip with friends to Alaska. The destination is a fishing lodge tucked in a cove on Prince of Wales Island in a setting that looks like something out of a National Geographic magazine. He loves this trip and counts down the days until the next time he would go. He described it as his "happy place" and said that the only thing missing was me. He is so sweet like that; always showing his love and letting me know that he wants us to spend more time together. As someone who doesn't fish, I had no interest in going in the past, but this time I say yes! It is not a cheap trip, and I'm thinking in the back of my mind, *I sure hope Justin is doing okay when I leave, because I refuse to cancel.* It seems like I'm always canceling something because of Justin.

The trip is scheduled over the 4th of July holiday, and we will be gone a week. Once I make my mind up to go, I get excited and can't wait to see the beauty of Alaska.

Dillon is in college attending Chico State University. Shay is living locally, and Justin is living at home. While I'm out of town, his job is to keep the house clean, water the plants, and take care of Maggie. From the time we adopted her, Maggie has always been afraid of loud noises, so it's important that someone be with her when the fireworks go off on the 4th of July, because she will completely freak out. She will either run or cower in the corner, trembling and whimpering at the sound of each blast. It's awful. She needs to be home and comforted. In the past, she seems to feel safest nestled under the covers in Dillon's bed, and I want that for her, so I pass on sending her to the kennel and take my chances on Justin. He seems to be functioning fairly well, but he doesn't look great. Frankly, at this point, I think I forgot what he looked like when he was doing good, so I convince myself it will be fine. I need a life. I want to spend some time with my boyfriend, and I want to get out of town. I want to eat good food, drink some wine, be in nature, and enjoy wide-open space. I desperately want to forget about everything.

Before leaving I review with Justin exactly what he is supposed to do. I write lists, give him instructions, and I leave some cash for food which is kind of a joke. I direct him, and I use the word "direct" intentionally, because I am really getting into a crazy level of detail. Anyway, the directive is to save the receipts from his food purchases so I could verify what he spent money on. I even provide a blue fabric zip up folder to put all the receipts in. Are you getting a picture of how I tried to control things all the way from Alaska? I am over the top. I give a few warnings and throw in some, "You better not screw this up" comments, and when all my lists are made and I have nothing left to say, I grab my stuff, jump in Darwin's truck, and we are off. All seems well, or at least I've convinced myself it is.

There is no cell service where we are going, but we do have Internet access. I try not to worry about it; what's the worst that could happen in a week?

We arrive at our destination and we're having a great time; the lodge is magical and in a setting that is just breathtaking. We watch whales breaching in the ocean, bald eagles flying overhead, and the lush greenery of Alaska surrounds us.

The food is beyond delicious, and I am ravenous. I'm sometimes a picky eater, and I always wonder about freshness. I'm constantly checking expiration dates, so to have fish from ocean to plate on the same day is really something. Fish, vegetables, and salad are served daily with good wine on the table every evening, as we all gather for dinner after the guys return from their long day of fishing. I eat crab until I can't eat any more, and I savor every bite. Darwin loves to see me eating so well and smiles as he watches me clean my plate every meal. We have mimosas in the morning, water with cucumber throughout the day, and it is delightful. This vacation is exactly what I needed.

Our little cabin is cozy and charming, and the people here are truly kind. I am able to relax and laugh and spend quality time with Darwin and some of our dearest friends; I am having a blast! Occasionally my mind drifts to Modesto, and I wonder what is going on at the house. When those thoughts come, I shake them off, telling myself to be present and enjoy every moment of this vacation.

Early in the mornings while Darwin is fishing, I get my exercise clothes on, put on my headphones, and run the steps around the lodge down to the dock where I can do my push-ups and get my workout in. Afterwards, I stretch out on the dock and look out at the peaceful morning, taking in the water's view that is as calm and still as glass that beautifully reflects the trees and clouds above me. It is simply glorious. The noise of the fishing boats setting out for the day is long gone, and the only sound is the occasional bird chirping. I feel calm in nature, and it reminds me of how big this world really is and how small mine has become. I pray and try my best to clear my mind and just "be."

One morning while Darwin is on the fishing boat and with my workout already done, I have a little time before my friend wakes up, so I check my Facebook page and see that I have a private message from Justin. He claims the house is great, everything is fine, but he is exhausted because he had been up all night with Maggie, who he claims is really sick. His writing is very detailed; it seems too detailed with lots of exclamation points, some "I love you and miss you" messages are included, and it sounds fake. I keep reading. He says he has taken Maggie to the vet around the corner at PetSmart® and needs money to get her medicine. As I read his words, I know he's lying. He continues in his message saying he called his Aunt Martha to get her advice on Maggie and to see if he could borrow some money to get her medicine. I'm instantly mortified. Is he using our dog as a means to get money? Or wait, could this be true? Is Maggie okay? I re-read his message and try to decipher it. We message back and forth and I get a sick feeling that this is all a lame attempt to get drug money. Aunt Martha gives him advice to help Maggie without the meds, and he says he will try it. I fight off the worry, the anger, the anxiety of wondering what is going on and pretend to enjoy the rest of our time.

Our trip comes to an end, and we say our goodbyes with a hope to come back next year; this trip and place would become one of my favorites. We hop on the float plane to Ketchikan at 6:00 a.m., take the water taxi to Seattle, and keep ourselves busy during the three-hour layover. I'm physically there with Darwin and our friends, but my mind is a thousand miles away.

We finally board our flight to Sacramento, getting close to the end of our 12-hour travel day. We make it to the truck and load our suitcases, backpacks and the one hundred pounds of fish he caught. We peel off our jackets, exchange our UGG® boots for flip flops and try to adjust to the 100-degree weather in Sacramento. With the air conditioner running full blast and the truck loaded, we start the final one and a half-hour drive home. The closer we get, the more anxious I become.

I'm back in cell service and see that I have three missed calls from Justin and a text message that says: "Hi, Mom! Hope you had a great time. When will you be home? Can't wait to see you!" I read it over and over again. He can't wait to see me? He's trying way too hard, and I know what that means. I feel sick to my stomach.

I have a message from Shay, so I call her back. She tells me her brother is acting "shady," and she's not sure what's going on. She's checked on the house, and it's fine, but something just doesn't seem right. By this time, my heart is racing.

We get to Escalon, where Darwin lives and where my car is parked. He asks if I want to come in for a minute, and I decline, saying I'm tired and ready to get home. He looks at me and knows he's already lost his fun loving, happy girlfriend that he caught a glimpse of in Alaska. But being the thoughtful, gentle man that he is, he doesn't ask any questions. He just wraps his arms around me, lays a kiss on my forehead, and pulls me into the comfort of his 6'4" frame. I love that he's so tall; sometimes when I feel like I can't stand on my own I know I can just lean on him, and he will support me. I pause for a moment in the safety of his arms, and then pull away and say goodbye. In my rear-view mirror, I see him standing in his driveway, watching me as I leave, and I wonder what he's thinking. I dismiss that thought and begin my drive home, hoping for the best and preparing for the worst.

I walk in the house, and Justin immediately approaches me, already overcompensating for what he knows is not going to be a pleasant encounter. I got worked up long before I walked in the door, and I think he senses it. He approaches me with a forced smile and an over-enthusiastic greeting "Hi, Mom! How was your trip?" I stop for just a second and look him over; Justin looks bad. His skin is pale, and his eyes look dull and lifeless. He reaches out as if he's going to hug me, and I push past him. The house is dark and dirty. The house I left spotless a week ago now looks filthy, and it's not just that it's dirty. I know that it's common when we leave our kids at home for us parents to return to a messy house, but that's not what I'm talking about. The house is dark somehow, it feels ugly to me. It is an eerie feeling; one I do not like at all.

I start yelling at him and throwing things around. I accuse Justin of being on drugs, of lying about Maggie, and I tell him what a piece of crap I think he is. He acts insulted and looks around in amazement as if something is happening "to" him; like he is somehow an innocent bystander in this battle he and I are in.

I go to the backyard and call for Maggie who trots up with her tail wagging to greet me. Her food bowl is full and she has fresh water. I stop and wonder if he filled her bowls up right before I got home. That's where my head was, I know how much Justin loves our dog, but he feels like a total stranger to me, and I trust nothing at this point.

I silently vow to never leave him alone in the house again, to get him out of my home and somehow out of my life. I feel disgusted by the whole mess, so I do what I always do and start cleaning, trying to get everything back in order. As I go to get my cleaning supplies I glance at the kitchen table and can't help but laugh. Not a joyful laugh but an "I'm an idiot" laugh because everything I left, the lists and the empty receipt folder are all in the same exact place on the table, left untouched, except of course for the money that was probably gone before we were even out of Modesto.

I turn the lights on, open windows, sweep our hardwood floors, scrub the bathrooms and kitchen, water the plants, and clean the patio. I'm in control again; my energy and rage are fading.

At some point, during the frenzy, Justin leaves, and I am grateful to be alone. I want nothing more than to go to the track and do my thing, but I don't feel comfortable leaving the house just yet and I'm exhausted. I take a shower and put my shorts and tank top on, turn on the cooler and sit in the living room looking around and wondering who may have been in my house and what happened while I was gone.

I rub Maggie's ears and love on her and wish she could talk to me. I tell her I'm sorry, and hug and kiss her until my guilt eases. She's fine; the house is back in order; I need to calm down and try to relax.

I think about the preparation for the trip and the endless talks I had with Justin. I think about how much time I've spent worrying about what was going on after I read his Facebook message and the painful trip home, where I was consumed with dark, agonizing thoughts about what he was up to. It occurs to me that Justin wasn't thinking about any of those things. His only use for me is shelter and money for drugs.

I flashed back to the look on his face when he saw the cash on the table; he paid no attention to anything I was saying. He was looking at that money like it was dinner and he was starving. I think about his message and consider that at that point, he must have run out of drugs and come up with the story about Maggie as an attempt to manipulate me or Aunt Martha into giving him money. His time was spent planning how to get his hands on more drugs; that's it. He didn't take care of our home; he didn't care about his responsibilities to our family, and he probably didn't even care about Maggie. Wow, this is getting clearer in my mind. I see it now; while I'm consumed with him and his well-being, all he's consumed with is getting high. The thoughts bring on a fresh wave of anger and despair.

All the beauty of the trip feels destroyed by the mess I've come home to. My tolerance is running out, and I am not sure if Justin has become a fake, conniving low-life, or if he is just deep in his drug addiction. I decide that it's probably both. I shut and lock the front door, tuck Maggie into Dillon's bed, and go to my room hoping Justin and the darkness he has brought to my life would just go away.

JUSTIN

I can't believe it's already been a week since Mom's been gone. I've been in a comfortable haze the entire time without anyone hassling me. I didn't miss the hundred questions a day, or the drug tests, or comments about how bad I look. I was able to do what I wanted and not worry about *anything*. She even left me money for food, which was enough to feed my habit for a few days.

Shay came by a few times, and I think I managed it ok. I'm sure Mom asked her to check on me, so I was careful to keep the house in order. She never stayed long, and I intentionally kept my distance. I did not want to deal with my sister thinking I was loaded.

I know Mom and Darwin are flying home from Alaska today, but I don't know what time. I start to panic. I call her several times, and there's no answer, so I text her, "Hi! Hope you had a great time. When will you be home? Can't wait to see you!" I read it over a few times before I press send. I think it sounds good; it sounds normal. I hope she's not on her way yet, because I need more time.

I take the last twenty dollars that I have and call my dealer. He's around the corner, so I tell him to just come to the house. I'm starting to feel sick and weak; I don't want to walk anywhere. He pulls up, I hand him the twenty dollars, and he gives me a bag. The sensation of it in my hand makes me feel better already. With new energy I run up the walkway into the house and shut and lock the door behind me. I use the entire bag all at once and let the warmth in; the relief is instant. I sink to the floor and lean against the couch trying to keep my eyes open long enough to feel my entire body become light, and then lighter, until I float away completely.

I hear Maggie whining, so I get up and let her out. I fill up her water dish and get her some food and look around the house, trying to see how it will look to Mom. I know it won't be perfect like she wants it. She wants everything perfect, but nothing is ever perfect enough for her anyway.

I check my phone and see a message: *I already told you I would be home this evening, why are you so worried about what time it will be? Just make sure the house is clean.*

That means she's back in cell service. I dread having to see her.

I take a shower and do my best with my appearance. I should be worried, but I don't really care anymore. If I get kicked out, so be it. I'm tired of dealing with her anyway.

I do a once over on the house and think it looks good. I take another look in the mirror and splash some cold water on my face, hoping it somehow helps my appearance.

Mom is home. I greet her at the door, "Hey Mom, how was your trip?" I try my best to smile and move in to hug her, but she's already looking right through me. She goes off and starts ranting about the house and that I look high. I stand back and just let her rant.

She makes her way to go see Maggie in the backyard, and I notice she left her purse on the floor. I quickly open her wallet and take a twenty out, put it in my pocket and slip her wallet back in its place and take off. I need to be anywhere but here.

"PLEASE STOP DOING DRUGS.
I BEG OF YOU.
I'M PLEADING.
I FEEL HOLLOW.
I'M ANGRY.
STOP! STOP RIGHT NOW!!!
I SCREAM IN YOUR FACE,
BUT YOU DON'T HEAR ME.
I'M ASHAMED OF YOU.
I HATE WHO YOU'VE BECOME.
YOUR ADDICTION IS TEARING
OUR FAMILY APART.
YOU'RE DESTROYING ME.
I KNOW I'M GOING TO LOSE YOU.
WHEN DID YOU BECOME SO WEAK?
WHY CAN'T YOU STOP?"

Kathryn Mae Inman

Counting Spoons

TRYING TO BREATHE

CHAPTER
NINE

KATHRYN

The pain in my chest, where my heart still manages to beat, is so real and strong that I wonder how I'm still alive. I'm walking through the day, putting one foot in front of the other but my mind is foggy. My nerves feel like a prickly cactus stinging my skin with every sound I hear.

I'm in the grocery store and see a friend, so I ditch my cart full of groceries and take off out of the store as fast as I can. I feel relief as soon as I sit in the safety of my vehicle. I wonder what the hell I'm running from? I left the store and my groceries because I just couldn't face her; she will see right through me. I scream at the top of my lungs and beat my fists against my steering wheel, and for a minute, I feel better. I don't care about the groceries, so I drive to the track, put my tennis shoes on, grab my ear buds, crank the music loud, and run the bleachers. I run up and down the stairs, kicking out twenty push-ups each round. Finally, after forty minutes, I make my last climb up to the top bleacher and sit, looking at the sky, and it's beautiful. My heart is pounding, I'm trying to catch my breath, and sweat is trickling down my back. I tell myself I'm going to be okay; I can handle this. My son may not survive, but I will. I'm strong; I've been through a lot, but I can do this. I will do this!

My confidence is short-lived because when I think of living in this world without Justin, it brings a wave of darkness that covers me like a blanket on a hot summer day. It's heavy and thick, and I feel like I might suffocate. I try to shake off the feeling and slowly jog back to the car.

My phone rings, and I don't recognize the number but answer it anyway; it's someone looking for Justin. I listen to the threats, "He owes me money. I know where you live; where is he?" Blah, blah, blah. I'm not in the mood for this. "Well, he owes me money too, so screw you!" I hang up. I'm not scared, I could not care less. All you addicted, drug dealing, shady people come at me! I don't care anymore. I am not tough by any means, but there is something dangerous about a person who is hanging by a thread, and I am definitely hanging on by a thread. It's a reckless feeling with the absence of any rational fear. I just feel numb to it all.

I made sure I had a baseball bat in my car and one in the corner of most every room in my house, so if I needed to protect myself I could. The jerk keeps calling back, so I throw my phone in the back seat and drive home. I walk into the house, drop my keys and purse on the floor, and flop down on my bed. My mind starts swirling like a blender full of bad thoughts and I wonder what will happen to us.

JUSTIN

Each day just keeps getting worse. I can't escape the sickness, so I'm trying to detox at home with Suboxone®. I owe people money, and I know they're looking for me. I don't think I can even fight anyone at this point; I'm too sick and weak.

I've convinced Mom that Suboxone is the answer, so she drove me to get some from a friend and is letting me detox at home. I tell her there are guys looking for me, but she doesn't seem to care. I put a bat by the front door just in case, and I curl up under the blankets wanting to die.

The loud knocking on the door wakes me up, and I'm shaking. My anxiety is bad. My sheets are soaked from my sweat. Mom walks into my room and looks at me, I shrink into my bed and pull the covers up over my head.

I hear the front door open, and then I hear yelling. What do I do now? I sneak into the dining room and peek out the window; it's him. Troy is here to collect the two hundred dollars I owe him. I lean against the wall and slide down to the floor, hiding. I hear my mom's voice raised and Troy yelling at her. I should go help her. I should take care of this. But I can't. I can't move or break through this sickness. I just want to die.

I crawl on the floor back to my room and get under the covers and hope Troy goes away. I wish I had one more bag; just a little more dope to take the edge off.

Counting Spoons

WHEN THE TRAIN HIT ME

CHAPTER
TEN

KATHRYN

Justin had been in his addiction for a while, and times were tough. Arguing, suspicion, tension, lies, and drama were always present, but I really didn't know what I was dealing with until our second visit to Kaiser.

Let me back up. I am at work, throwing myself into my job like I always did to provide for my family. I hold a high-level position with a lot of responsibility, and my home life is in complete chaos; all the chaos that comes with addiction. I'm at my desk and get a call from my neighbor, Michelle, who tells me my son and his friend Brent are taking garbage bags of stuff out of my house and loading it into Brent's car. Justin and Brent played baseball together, and I heard Brent was heavily into drugs. I tell Michelle I'm on my way. I close up my office and try to mask how angry I already am as I'm exiting the building. I drive home in two minutes; it usually takes five. I pull up to my street, slam on my breaks, and come to a tire-screeching stop right in front of Brent's car.

I jump out and take off in a full sprint in my work heels, grab the bag out of Brent's hands and rip it open to find my shoes, clothes, and other personal belongings. I stare at my stuff in disbelief and realize they're stealing from me. They were intending to sell my personal belongings for drug money! By this point, I'm feeling adrenaline at a level that can only be described as blind rage. I start screaming at him to leave and then run into the house to find Justin, fresh out of the shower acting like all is well. I blow up. I'm losing it, and he's trying to calm me down which just agitates me more.

I frantically look around my house, running from room to room, trying to inventory my belongings. I find another garbage bag in the backyard with more of my clothes and shoes in it, including my favorite pair of army green pants, brand-new black heels, and my slip-on comfy shoes with rainbow-colored leather straps. I kick him out. I'm done and I am furious.

I hand him a bottle of water and a pillow and tell him to get out or I'm calling the cops. He asks for his brass knuckles, which I won't give him, and he yells, "How am I supposed to protect myself?"

First, it's a felony to even own brass knuckles, and second, I could not care less whether he's protected. I remember thinking people need to be protected from him, not the other way around. I tell him to go sleep at the mission or in a park; just go before I call the cops. He finally leaves.

My heart is racing; I feel no sadness, no remorse, no worry, just pure, raw rage at the violation of what just happened. I don't sleep a wink; I lie emotionless and stare at the ceiling.

JUSTIN

I'm just out of the shower, when I hear Mom yelling. I panic. Why is she home?! Brent is out in his car, and we were just getting ready to leave. I walk to the garage, and here she comes, running at me. This is bad. "Mom, Mom, Mommmm! Calm down!" She just keeps coming at me and pushes me against the wall. I try to get her to stop yelling, but she won't. I look for Brent but don't see him; I ask her where he is.

"I made him leave! You're stealing my stuff?! What is wrong with you?" This is so bad. I don't know what to do.

She walks in the house and starts completely losing it. "You've been taking my clothes and shoes all this time! What is wrong with you? You are sick, you're a terrible person, Justin!" What do I say?

I'm so busted. I just look at her. She goes in the backyard, and I stand there and close my eyes, hoping she doesn't see the bag I hid back there because it's full of her stuff. She finds it and comes barreling back into the house.

"Get out of my house, Justin."

"Mom, please, no, I'm sorry, I can explain. I just need a minute, Mom, please!"

She looks at me with what feels like genuine hate. She repeats herself, talking slowly, "Get out of my house now, before I call the cops."

Oh man, she's serious. I have nowhere to go, and I'm going to be sick soon. I have no idea where Brent is, and I don't have my phone anymore. I panic. "Mom, PLEASE! Can we just talk?" She tells me to get out. "Where am I supposed to go?"

"I don't care where you go, Justin, do you hear me? Sleep at the Mission for homeless, or sleep in a park, I don't care! Just go!"

I start to walk toward my room, and she blocks me. I tell her I need my brass knuckles for protection, but she won't give them to me. She gives me a bottle of water and a pillow.

I have no dope, no money, no phone. Withdrawals are creeping into my bones, and I can't be on the street because people are looking for me. I ride my bike to the shelter and get a number like all the other homeless people. It's one of the worst nights of my life. I want to crawl out of my skin. I keep my papers so I have proof that I came to the shelter and hope that somehow knowing I spent a night there will soften her up enough to let me come back home. I don't know what to do. I don't know how to stop using, and I'm scared of being dope sick. How did I get here? I have to do something; I have to get well again. I can't take this. My own mother can't stand the sight of me. I need help. I'm fading into nothing. I want my life back.

KATHRYN

At 7:00 a.m. the next morning, Justin comes back to the house with a paper showing he slept at the mission, and I remember thinking, why is he giving me proof? Weird. Anyway, he tells me he's ready to

Counting Spoons

get help, and a little part of me grabbed on to hope. PLEASE let this be a new beginning.

I call work and tell them I'll be out of the office for the day, and we head to Kaiser. I can see that the night in a shelter has rattled Justin. He's red-faced, and his veins are pulsing, but he's not high. He seems in shock that he finds himself in this place and looks like he might cry. We go to Kaiser, and he signs up for outpatient treatment. I talk to my boss and arrange for a flexible schedule so I can take him three times a week for six weeks. He tells me, "Everything I need is here. It's great Mom; I'll be okay," and I believe him.

He's now eighteen and an adult, which changes the game, to some degree. Things continue to escalate at home, and we find ourselves in the same situation; he's using daily, but this time, on the second ride to Kaiser I've gotten a little smarter and demand to go in with him. He says no, so I tell him either he signs a paper that gives me access to all his records and information or he's on the streets. He knows I mean it, so he signs all the papers, and we walk in to see the doctor.

He's clearly dope-sick and full of anxiety; he looks terrified. I try to focus on the doctor as she is running through the typical questions: "How long have you been using? How many milligrams? When did you last use heroin?" And then everything stopped. Wait just a minute. I raise my hand into the air as if signaling her to stop "Whoa, whoa, wait a minute, what? I thought we were talking about pills?" I look frantically at the doctor and then at Justin, and he quickly looks down. I am in complete shock.

My thoughts are racing... heroin is the drug that junkies used back in the 60's. But my son is not a junkie. This is my kid! That's when the train hit; the train that I did not see coming just ran me over. My son is a heroin addict. For the love of God how did this happen?

My mind is reeling. I hold my head in my hands, and the doctor asks if I need a minute. Without looking up, I tell her in a louder than expected voice, "YES, I NEED A MINUTE." She leaves for about ten minutes. I look at Justin and he looks away. We sit in silence as I try to get my head around this new information. The doctor walks back in and asks, "Are we ready to proceed?" I look at this twenty something beautiful, tall, thin, polished doctor who is just doing her job, and I can't help but feel the coldness. This is routine. She does it every day and deals with parents and patients just like me and Justin all the time. BUT THIS IS MY KID! I want to scream at the top of my lungs, THIS IS JUSTIN! He was meant for so much more! But I don't say any of those things. I just say, "Yes, we are ready to proceed."

Justin is a mess and getting sick, so they load us up with meds to go home and detox, and we do that for three days. It's like living in hell; watching him sick and trying to detox was horrible. Anxiety, sweats, nausea, diarrhea, deep in the bones kind of muscle aches, and inability to sleep or eat. I imagine it feels like a terrible flu, only one hundred times worse. By the fourth day, he's holding food down, and we start putting one foot in front of the other. A few weeks go by, and I can tell he's high again. We argue, and I give him a choice; get help or get out, and then we head back to Kaiser once again. I tell the doctor, "He's a heroin addict, and he's not allowed back in my house, so either we get him in some kind of inpatient facility, or he's on the street." There is no crack in my voice, no tears, or hesitancy. From the outside, I might have even appeared calm.

The same doctor is helping us; she looks at me and says, "You're different than you were last time you were here," and I respond, "Yep, I am." She looks at me and holds her gaze, and I stare right back at her determined not to blink or look down. I'm thinking, what the hell are you staring at me for? What are you trying to see?! I'm angry and I don't have any tears left; is that what you see? After what feels like an eternity, she looks away, and I think I see a shade of approval on her face, but I'm not sure. She asks about the mark on his face, and in my mind, I dare him to tell the truth. Tell the doctor I slapped you and left a mark Justin; go ahead and tell her, because I don't care. I'll do it again. I love you so much son, and I hate you more than I can even admit. Why aren't you strong enough to do this? Why can't you handle this? When did you become so weak? I remain silent and lock my eyes on his; he looks at me and lies and tells her he scraped his face on something. The beautiful Doctor exits, and Justin and I don't speak.

She comes back and assigns us a counselor and gets him a bed for inpatient detox in Stockton. Now we're talking. Inpatient! I get to take him somewhere to get help and leave him there. What I didn't realize

Counting Spoons

was this was the first of five trips to this same detox center. I'm glad I didn't know that then; it would have broken me.

That day I dropped him off, I remember relief flooding my body as I was driving home. I thought we were finally getting somewhere and had no idea that this nightmare was just beginning.

JUSTIN

My anxiety is terrible. I need relief! I wish I had some dope. Well, now Mom knows her precious son is a heroin addict. The look on her face when she found out I'm using heroin made me feel like a lowlife. I know she thinks I'm nothing but a disappointment. Whatever. I just want to feel normal again. Once I get past the withdrawals, I'll be okay, and then I'll show everyone who I really am. I just need to stop using. If I can just get through the sickness, I'll be okay. I've got this. I can handle it.

"HOPE AND FEAR CANNOT OCCUPY
THE SAME SPACE AT THE SAME
TIME. INVITE ONE TO STAY."

Maya Angelou

ONE DAY AT A TIME

CHAPTER
ELEVEN

KATHRYN

Justin calls; he's five days into detox, and I can already hear the difference in his voice. There is no heaviness in his tone and no slurring. I feel instant relief; it's been quite some time since I've heard his voice sound so clear. I'm always surprised at how quickly my heart shifts for my son. When he's using, he is like a complete stranger, and I hate him; nothing about the addicted Justin is familiar to me. He doesn't look, act, or seem like the same person. But my true son—the clean, sober, clear-minded Justin, I love with all my heart and would do anything for. I take a long, deep breath and try to stay in the present and not worry about tomorrow. He is clean, and that's all that matters right now. We are going to take this one day at a time.

Justin apologizes for everything that's happened and is anxious to try and piece his life back together. He asks if I can bring him some chapstick and snacks when I come to visit, and I tell him I will. His voice sounds small when he asks how Dillon, Shay, and Maggie are doing. I assure him they are fine; we all just want him to get better. It's quiet on the phone, and he sounds frail. "I know Mom, me too." I imagine being clear-minded is hard for Justin. He's likely thinking about all the bad things he's done and wondering if we have had enough. And we have, we've all had enough. But we still love him and will support him.

We talk about next steps because I won't allow him to come back home. He will be released from detox in two days, and then he will go to a rehab facility called the "Pink House" in San Jose, California. He will stay there for thirty days of inpatient treatment, and from there he can move into a sober living house.

I talk to the insurance company representative and get the details of what he needs to bring and what paperwork we need to fill out. I am instructed to pick him up and go straight to the Pink House and not make any stops along the way. Got it. I feel like I'm transporting a prisoner.

Justin makes it through the thirty days at the Pink House, and he looks great. He's gained weight; his eyes are clear, and his face has color again. Darwin, my sister (his Aunt Martha), his Uncle Ed, and I head to his graduation. As we walk in, I immediately spot him and watch how he is interacting with others. I notice how people are drawn to him. He seems to have made friends and figured out how to navigate through the program successfully; good for him.

During the ceremony, the counselor calls up each graduate, hands them their certificate of completion and asks if they'd like to say a few words to their family members. Justin spoke, and I could tell it was heartfelt. I see the tears in his eyes as he apologizes for all he put us through. I'm feeling relieved that this nightmare is over and grateful to have my son back. As I look around the room at the other graduates, I feel like my son doesn't belong here; he just doesn't look like he fits in.

During the family group sessions, the counselor keeps emphasizing that relapse is a common part of the recovery process, and I am annoyed by that. There is no way Justin would put our family through this again. Justin is different from the others in here; circumstances happened, he experimented with drugs, and like everything else he does, he took it too far, and it got a grip on him. He is not like the others in this place. In retrospect, I wonder if everyone in the room was thinking the same way about their loved one.

I remember one family in particular. The guy in the program is in his thirties but looks a lot older. His name is Dave, and he is battling alcoholism. It is a "family only" group session, meaning the participants of the program are not present. The counselor is coaching us on what to expect from our loved ones now that they have at least thirty days of sobriety under their belt. Dave's brother and their parents are here. Dave's mom and dad look weary, but his brother just looks pissed, and I'm wondering what he's thinking. I am about to find out, because he raises his hand when the counselor asks if anyone has questions. His brother stands up; he's a big, muscular guy with a clean-shaven head. He asks, "When do we get to call him out on all the crap he's put us through? When do I get to lay into him about what he's done to my parents?!"

This guy is saying what everyone else is probably thinking, and I totally get where he's coming from. What about our pain? I already know the response he's about to get from the counselor.

"Actually, it's better not to rub his face in the mistakes he's made; believe me it haunts him every minute. He doesn't need to be reminded." The room is quiet; Dave's brother sits down but I can tell he's not happy.

With the graduation over, it's time to move into the sober living house. I pick up Justin with my car loaded with food, toiletries, bedding, and enough clothes to get him settled. He's allowed one cupboard and one shelf in the refrigerator for his food; I pack it full.

Justin moves in, and I pay his first month's rent with the understanding that he will get a job and support himself, which he does. He's had experience working on cars, and lands a job as a mechanic making pretty decent money. It's a great start, and it seems like things are going well.

I hear from Justin daily. He loves his job and is making it work at the house but is anxious to get his own place soon. He tells me about a guy that got kicked out after getting caught shooting heroin in the closet the night before. I don't respond, but the thought that Justin was in the same room with heroin makes me feel sick.

I meet him for lunch at his favorite Vietnamese restaurant that's right next to the shop where he works. They know him well and seem excited to meet me. They give us a free appetizer and make sure we are taken care of. I marvel at how quickly Justin makes an impression on people. Things seem to be falling into place for him, and just when I think we're going to be okay, everything crumbles.

Justin earns a weekend pass and comes home with a friend for the weekend. They go out to a party and drink. Unbelievable. I am fuming. I know what's going to happen next, and it does. He fails the urine test and is immediately exited from the program. He couch-hops for a while until he finds a room to rent and then things start to go downhill quickly. I can hear the strain in his voice, and I know he's using again. *What the hell are we gonna do now?*

Things escalate, and we find ourselves driving back to the same detox for the second time in less than a year. I hear the counselor's voice in my head saying, "relapse is part of the recovery process," and I think it's crap; I think it's weak, and I'm sick of it.

Kaiser finds another program in San Jose called the Amicus house, and Justin goes there after detox. This is the last program insurance will pay for. He seems committed and it sounds like he's making some progress. His counselor shares with me that he's the most challenging person she's ever worked with, and I'm not sure what to say to her, so I don't say anything at all.

He stays for thirty days, and then Kaiser approves another thirty days, as we are waiting for an opening at a program called Teen Challenge. Connie from the insurance company has worked with us from the beginning, and she thinks Justin might do well at Teen Challenge. It's a faith-based program and they have a good success rate. It's also a twelve-month program, and I like the sound of that. Thirty days were not enough; he needs something more.

Justin has had all his privileges taken away at the Amicus house because he keeps breaking rules and has had a conflict with some of the participants. One young man couldn't seem to get along with Justin. His name was Dan. He was a tall, thin kid with long dark hair that hung in his face, covering his pale skin. I learned Dan struggled with both addiction and mental illness, and I wondered how his parents managed. Dan seemed obsessed with Justin and talked a lot about him in his counseling sessions, and that caused some concern among the counselors. Eventually Dan started having issues with everyone in the program and ended up leaving unexpectedly early. We later found out he committed suicide within a week of going home. The news hits everyone hard, and Justin is visibly shaken. I realize how fragile life is. My heart breaks for his parents that I'm sure, like me, were trying everything they could to save their son, but it just wasn't enough. I hate the darkness that covers families that are struggling with addiction.

On a Saturday during visiting hours, Martha and I drive out to meet Justin and bring him lunch. It is a good visit, but everyone seems subdued; still trying to process the recent tragedy. We leave; I drop Martha off and don't remember the rest of my drive home as I'm deep in thought about all the pain and suffering that seems to swallow up these young adults. They all have stories. There is a young woman just twenty years old that had her newborn taken away from her because her baby was born addicted; she also has a two-year-old that her grandma is taking care of while she gets clean. There is a young man with decaying teeth who has been in and out of rehabs for the past five years, and another boy who was disowned by his family for all the bad things he has done in his addiction; he is facing significant time in jail once he graduates from this program. I picture my son amongst all these broken people and can't help but wonder how we ended up here; I never saw this coming.

Justin gets his blood work done for Teen Challenge and submits his application, gets accepted, and now we must wait for a bed to open. The insurance company will not extend his stay at the Amicus House, and there are no beds open at Teen Challenge, so we have a dilemma. Justin sleeps in his car a few nights and then finds a room to rent, and I agree to pay for it, hoping he will get a bed at Teen Challenge soon. Justin gets settled in the new room, and I buy him a whole new set of bedding, toiletries, and food. The last person locked Justin out of the house and kept all his belongings and I didn't have it in me to try to deal with it, so we just left everything there.

Justin is attending outpatient drug treatment classes daily, and I'm hoping he can stay clean until we get him to the next program. I finally receive the call that they have an opening at Teen Challenge in Sacramento, and he needs to arrive tonight. I'm happy there's an opening, but curious why everything is so urgent in these programs, when there is a bed you must come right then. It hits me that a lot of people need these services and I immediately feel like crying.

It is nine o'clock at night and storming outside, but I'm determined to get him into this year-long program because I know he needs it. I call the facility where he's attending classes, halfway expecting them to tell me they've never heard of him, but he's there in class, so they pull him out, and he comes to the phone. Justin sounds thrilled at the news and agrees to pack his stuff and be ready when I get there.

We make it to Sacramento Teen Challenge in good time. It's in a nice neighborhood with beautiful trees lining the streets. Justin will stay there for thirty to forty-five days, graduate, and then move to the next phase of the program in Southern California. This is a faith-based program, and Justin is open to it. I think about him turning to the Lord for strength and it's encouraging.

It's early on a Saturday morning when I check the mailbox; there is a thick envelope waiting for me. It's a letter from Justin. I quickly get settled on the couch with a cup of coffee and read...

"Two days of being here, and they made me "the cook!"
So, every morning I have to get up by 4:45 a.m.,
shower, get dressed, and have breakfast ready by 7:00
a.m. It's for twenty-one guys so I have a helper. His
name is Corey, and he's from Nevada. He's twenty-
three and attracted to me, which actually works out
great because he really, really likes me, which means
whatever I need him to do, he does, and when he's
finished, he asks me what to do next! He's great. He
just cuts up veggies and does the dishes because he
can't cook. Anyway, after breakfast we have chores
from 8:30 to 9:00, from 9:00 to 10:00 we have
curriculum, from 10:00 to 11:00 Bible study, from
11:00 to 12:00 work hall, 12:00 to 1:00 I make lunch,
1:00 to 4:00 work hall, 4:00 to 6:00 I make dinner,
7:00 to 8:30 we have church, and in bed with lights
out at 9:00, lol! The schedule is intense. I've already
read about half of the Bible, and I've memorized ten
scriptures. It's ridiculous how much work there is.
But I'm doing very good. I'm ahead on all of my work;
my meals are delicious, and I'm always on time. I'm
so happy I went to the Amicus House first, because

I would have gone through hell here if I didn't. It's crazy, I'm the youngest guy here, and I'm the only one without a disciplinary write-up. I have the most responsibilities, and I'm doing great. It's amazing how much easier everything is after I changed my attitude and behavior. I have some friends here. I mostly kick it with Adam, he's twenty, Peter, twenty-six, and Oley, twenty-six. They are "re-entry" students. Meaning they have been in the program for thirteen months, so they come live here and help for an additional four months. Besides them, I don't really hang out with any students; some weird people are here too.

There are some old guys here that don't like me because I'm a 19-year-old, and I can't tell them what to do . . . my response was, you put yourself here! It's funny because I don't feel bad whatsoever; for the first time I'm showing some integrity. I've been given some responsibilities in the house; with specific rules the clients need to follow. So, when staff isn't around, all the clients think they can do whatever they want because a 19-year-old can't tell them what to do. NEWS FLASH BRO!!!I can, and I will! Ha!

I'm going absolutely nuts living with all these guys here, so I really look forward to church! The church is HUGE, and there are some fine women! One girl specifically. I always sit on the far-right front seat, she sits on the far-left front seat, and the pastor speaks in the middle. I'm pretty sure she is looking at me. Not totally sure yet...it could be the Pastor. But it seems like she is looking a few inches to the right of the Pastor, which would be looking at me...lol, I get a little stir crazy in this place but overall, it's going good. I'm telling you, there is something to this "God" thing. I'm enjoying learning and growing spiritually. It's just crazy how it's all happening. Thank you so much, Mom, for the package. I've been missing you and Dillon and Sis soooo much, and it really made me feel at home. That necklace is the best gift I've ever gotten, I'll keep it forever! Thank you sooooooooooo much! I need another chain though; I broke mine when I was lifting weights. I've been fitting in workouts about five days a week, and I feel healthier than ever. I've been running a lot, and since I quit tobacco, I have so much more energy. I can go and go and go! We have a scale; when I got here, I was 185 lbs. I was 191 lbs. this morning! Since I'm the cook and I'm doing good, I'm going to basically be able to choose where I want to go after this, and they said they will let you and Dillon take me there! I can call you when I find out. I missed you guys on Thanksgiving! I hope it was good for you guys. It was a different one for me, but also one of the best! I was able to make a 22-lb. turkey with stuffing, green bean casserole, corn, salad, rolls, and cranberry sauce; it was bomb. It was a cool experience. I love and miss you guys big time and can't wait to see you. Write back. If not, I'll call you when I find out where I'm going! Love, Justin."

Oh, Justin. My funny, sweet, ridiculous child. I read his letter over and over again, all the while smiling. I carefully fold it and put it back in the envelope so Dillon can read it when he gets home. I love how he sounds. I love that he cooked Thanksgiving dinner for all the guys there. I love that he wrote us a four-page letter, and, most importantly, I love that he is making this work.

He ends up making it through the forty-five days and commits his life to Christ. Amen for that. He needs all the help he can get.

Time passes quickly and now he's ready for the next phase of the program, and much to his delight, the location is San Diego, California. Dillon and I pick him up and get him on a bus to San Diego. This will be his home for the next six months.

Justin does well and is continuing his spiritual walk. Darwin and I make the drive for a Teen Challenge family picnic on the beach in Southern California, to witness Justin's second baptism. His first was when he was just a year old. Back then, he wore a white collared shirt with white shorts, and he was the cutest little thing. As the pastor sprinkled his head with water, I remember Justin looking up and giving him a big smile. The congregation laughed at the charming little boy that seemed to be basking in the attention of the ceremony. Now that little boy was a grown man of almost twenty years. His curly hair has grown out, and his body is once again muscular and tan. Justin is waist deep in the water with the pastor; as he dips in and comes back up, I see him searching for me, and we meet eyes. Justin gives me a smile, and I can almost hear what he's thinking. "I'm doing good now, Mom. Do you see me? Are you watching?" And I do see him.

The six months pass, and he continues to thrive; now it's time for his graduation. Martha and I fly to San Diego, check into our room, and call a taxi to take us to the ceremony.

As we're riding the elevator down to meet our taxi, Martha asks if I'm okay, and I tell her I am. Martha looks at me with concern on her face and says, "I'm asking because I can see your heart beating through your shirt." I look down and see it too; my shirt moving to the thumping of my heart. I take a deep breath and try to calm down. Another graduation for Justin. God, please let this be the last one. I hear the phrase again, "Relapse is a common part of the recovery process," and I wonder if there's a number of relapses that is common, or do people just relapse for the rest of their miserable lives. My nerves are shot.

We climb into the taxi. The driver is a really nice guy. We give him the address and begin the short drive to the ceremony. He asks us the standard questions; where are you from, what brings you here, and so forth, and I answer him. I proceed to tell him exactly why we are here and what Justin has been through, and barely take time to breathe between sentences. Martha is looking at me in utter shock. I'm shocked as well. I'm not sure where that all came from, but I just told this cab driver more information about Justin than I've told anyone. Martha looks at me and raises her eyebrows, and I just shrug and look out the window feeling tired suddenly. I never know how I'm going to handle things from one minute to the next; I feel like I'm always on edge.

The story left an impression on our cab driver because he promised to hang close and pick us up when we're done, which was great news because we had no clue how to get around in this town.

As we get closer, I become more anxious. I haven't seen Justin in a few months, and for some reason I keep thinking about the last ride we had to detox. He was high as a kite and nodding out, and I slapped him hard across the face. I could barely stand the sight of him. I didn't spank my kids. I never put my hands on them except in affection. They never needed that kind of discipline, so for me to slap him like that shocked both of us. He looked at me in horror and yelled at me to never touch him again "not even a hug" he said. I remember the feeling, and it was an awful kind of emptiness. It doesn't seem right to actually hate someone you love, but I did. I hated the addicted Justin. I shake away the thought and watch the streetlights out of the window of the cab, wondering what it will be like when I see Justin tonight. I say a quick prayer that it goes well.

We walk in the front doors, and Justin is standing there waiting for us. He looks like a little kid with that huge smile on his face. He doesn't hesitate at all; he runs up and wraps his arms around me and whispers "Man, Mom, it's so good to see you," and I feel the same. Relief and love flood over me as we hold on tightly to each other for a few more seconds, and then he's got Aunt Martha wrapped in his arms. This is the Justin I know and love. The Justin with the clear eyes that sparkle with mischief, the wide grin that sits permanently on his face, and the laugh that I love so much. This is the son I raised.

We watch the ceremony, and it's touching. These graduates have worked hard on their recovery and their walk-in faith. Now they will be moving on to the Riverside location for the final months of the program. Justin spends most of the night introducing us to people and making sure that his Aunt Martha and I have punch and cookies to our hearts content. I watch him as he works his way around the room talking to people, opening doors, moving chairs, and helping however he can. I reflect on other programs he's been in since this all started, and it's the same every time. I guess Justin is good at rehab.

I get introduced to friends that Justin has made in these programs, and often hear what an amazing guy he is. People have always been drawn to him. I remember one young man coming up to me and hugging me tightly. His eyes were full of tears, and in a voice, heavy with emotion, he told me he didn't think he would have made it through this program if it wasn't for Justin; "Your son is one of the best guys I've ever known." I wonder what it is about Justin that makes such a lasting impression on people, and I'm confused about whether this is a good thing or a bad thing. Is he having too much fun in rehab? I mentioned it to Dillon, and his response was, "Justin's *always* the man, Mom, wherever he goes." I ponder that for a moment and realize he's right. Justin's always been that way; why would it be any different in rehab?

Aunt Martha takes a few pictures, which Justin is happy to pose for. He flexes a few times, does a little dance, and gets his buddies to pose with him. We're having a good time; I almost forget the reason we are here.

We call the nice taxi guy, and he says he will be here in ten minutes. Justin asks permission to walk us out, and his counselor tells him yes; "See your family off Justin, take your time buddy." We walk out with Justin between me and my sister, with his arms stretched around each of our shoulders. He always does that. He's very affectionate, and I love that about him.

Justin walks up to the taxi driver and introduces himself and shakes his hand. He asks him to please get us back to the hotel safely and tells him that his mom and aunt are "precious cargo." I see the taxi driver looking at Justin trying to figure out if it's the same son I was telling him about on the ride here. I can almost hear what he's going to say as soon as Justin leaves, because there is no sign of the drug addict that he was just eight short months ago. We say our goodbyes, and it's hard to leave. I'm holding back tears, and Justin sees it; he assures me he will be fine. He thanks us for coming and tells us both he loves us. As we start to leave, Justin turns, taps on the hood and yells for us to "be safe," and then he jogs slowly back across the street and spins around to wave one more time before he opens the door and goes back inside.

The taxi driver talks the entire way back to the hotel. He is impressed by what a handsome, courteous young man my son is. "That one is going to be okay; that young man right there is going to be just fine." He glances at me in the rear-view mirror and gives me a quick wink. I smile in appreciation and hope to God he's right.

This next phase of the program is important because they will be helping Justin figure out how to cope in the real world, outside the protection of the program. I realize that my son is getting good at these programs; it's the outside world that he's got to figure out.

We arrive at the hotel, and since we're in beautiful San Diego, Martha and I decide to delay going to our room and take a walk to see the sites and get some ice cream. It's a nice break, and the fresh air feels good. We walk along the streets that are lit up and watch the people on skates and bikes as they pass us by. It's beautiful.

Tomorrow we will fly back home, and life will go on. Justin has just four months left before his final graduation, and then maybe we can start to work on being a family again. I sleep soundly and wake up feeling refreshed. I miss my son already but part of me wishes he could stay in this program and in a controlled environment forever. I know it's a silly thought because I really do want so much more for him, but the possibility of another relapse is just too much to think about, so I try my best not to. I remember Justin's counselor saying to "take one day at a time" and even though she was talking to Justin, I think it's good advice for me as well. One day at a time, one foot in front of the other, that's all I can do.

"THERE ARE FAR, FAR BETTER
THINGS AHEAD THAN ANY
WE LEAVE BEHIND."

C.S. Lewis

Counting Spoons

HE'S ON THE OUTSIDE

CHAPTER
TWELVE

KATHRYN

Life is looking brighter. Justin has almost completed the Teen Challenge program and will be graduating from Riverside in November 2013. He has thirteen months of sobriety, and he seems to be thriving. Since his addiction started, this is the longest he has been clean, and I'm feeling hopeful. My mind is allowing me to focus on the present and not the darkness of the past, and I'm grateful for that.

Thirteen months clean; I roll that around in my mind a bit. That equals 56 weeks away from the darkness, 395 days in the light, 9,480 hours of sobriety, and 568,800 minutes with a clear mind. I think about the time span. It's not that long, but it's a solid start. He can do this. I feel like I have my son back, and I cannot lose him again. I try to let go of any anxious thoughts and lean into the joy of his accomplishments and imminent graduation.

Over the last thirteen months, Justin and I speak often on the phone and write letters to each other, and I like what I am hearing from him. He seems to be learning compliance, and self-control. He sounds strong. He's studying the Bible, working long days, and taking good care of himself. He always has a lot to say, and sounds happy. He can feel joy again; he's no longer numb and empty inside. I had almost forgotten the free spirited, adventurous boy that is rising to the surface again. I really like this Justin; it's good to have him back.

Time goes by quickly, and we begin the conversations about what will happen after graduation. Justin's plan is to move in with a man named Marco, who he met in Teen Challenge; he is working on his recovery as well. Marco has a beautiful, loving wife and an amazing young son that seems drawn to Justin. They play baseball together every Sunday after church. Justin coaches him on how to swing the bat and field grounders; they play, laugh, and hang out together and it is special. Marco has a nice home in Southern California with a spare bedroom where Justin can live. Justin and Marco spent a lot of time together in the program, and Marco has confidence in Justin's athletic abilities. He thinks Justin could have a future in baseball and has encouraged him to walk-on and play at Cal State Fullerton. He is convinced Justin would make it far in the game just like Dillon. This seems like a promising plan. He would be out of Modesto, living with a good family, going to school, and he would be part of a team again. It makes sense to me, and Justin seems excited.

Unfortunately, before graduation everything changes. Justin received a phone call from Marco's wife saying that he had relapsed, and their family was devastated and trying to work through it. Marco ended up calling me as well and apologized profusely; he did not see this coming, and he needed to work on his own recovery. "I'm so sorry Kathryn, we're all upset about this but it's just not the right time for Justin to stay with us. Really, I am so terribly sorry, I hope you can forgive me." Of course, I can forgive him; this man obviously has a lot to deal with. It rattles me how quickly Marco's world has crumbled, and I realize now that I have a tough decision to make. After much consideration, I decide that Justin can stay at home with us just until he can get on his feet again. It will be a temporary living situation, and we were all clear on that.

The time comes for Justin's graduation. Dillon and I pack an overnight bag and begin the 365-mile drive to Riverside to attend the ceremony. I'm excited, happy, scared, proud, and anxious.

The graduation is powerful. Dillon and I listen to the testimony of several graduates, and I'm surprised by the struggle and pain these men have endured. I'm also happy to see the faces of the families of these men who, like me, look relieved that this day has finally come.

We are all anxious to close this chapter in life and move on to happier times.

After the ceremony, we meet some of Justin's closest friends, eat from a big spread of food, and watch as Justin says his goodbyes, and then we get in the car and head home.

Justin's in a good place emotionally. He seems calm and excited for the simple things that life offers. With the music blasting and windows down, we pull into a drive through for a burger and fries. Justin looks pleased. I imagine the little taste of freedom feels good to him. As if reading my thoughts, he glances in my direction and gives me a big smile, turns the radio up even more and starts singing to the music. My heart feels light and hopeful.

The six and a half-hour drive goes fast. Justin is quiet as he walks through the house and looks around. I'm sure ugly memories are flashing through his mind, but we all do our best to keep it light and be supportive of each other.

I run to the store to get a few things and get a call from Dillon saying that two guys came to the house asking to borrow money. These were two known addicts that Justin had partied with before. I was shocked. We hadn't even been home one day, and this crap is already starting? I rush home and am ready to rip Justin to shreds, but he meets me at the door and looks at me with his clear eyes.

"Mom, let's talk."

Dillon, Justin, and I sit down in the living room. I'm sitting on my hands, so they don't see me shaking. Justin explains that he had nothing to do with this; he had no idea those guys were coming over, and he hasn't talked to them in over a year. I look at him, listen to his words, and believe he's telling the truth. I start to compose myself.

Justin goes on to say that he had been cautioned by his counselors that situations like this would come up and that he would have to deal with them as honestly and calmly as possible. The grip of the past would continue its hold on him for a while. Our family still has a lot of healing to do.

Dillon got rid of the guys and ended up chasing them down again with a warning not to return to our house; explaining that his little brother is clean now and doesn't need any distractions.

We get past the incident quickly, but it is a harsh reminder that this journey is far from over; it will take some time for us to be able to trust him again.

Thanksgiving arrives, and it is beautiful. I spend hours preparing for our family to join us for an amazing feast. I look around the table, feeling nothing but gratitude to have my family together again; happy and healthy. Watching Justin laughing and carrying on while devouring the mountain of food on his plate brings me so much joy that I feel on the edge of tears the entire day. Grateful just doesn't seem like a strong enough word, but every ounce of me is present this Thanksgiving, soaking in the smells of good food and the sound of a family enjoying a holiday together. Justin offers to help me clean up, and we work together in a comfortable silence—feeling close again. As we're cleaning, my mind drifts back to the many times I've cleaned this same kitchen.

I remember when the boys were young; I would get up extra early on a soccer day to make them their favorite breakfast. I loaded the table full of pancakes, scrambled eggs, bacon, a bowl of fruit, and cinnamon rolls. The boys often had friends over, and I was determined that each tummy would be full before they left my house. Justin was usually the first one up. He would appear in the kitchen, rubbing his sleepy eyes. Then he would see the spread, gasp, cover his mouth dramatically and run down the hall yelling, "Guys! Wake up, wait until you see what Mom made us for breakfast! Come quick!" Then he'd run back to the kitchen and start filling his plate, wanting to get his food first. I smile at the memory as Justin and I finish cleaning the kitchen, a sweet ending to this beautiful Thanksgiving holiday.

Following Thanksgiving, comes a big move. After dating and being in a committed relationship for about fifteen years, Darwin and I decide to move in together. We know this would be a temporary place, as we were soon to be empty nesters, so we opt to rent a big two-story, five-bedroom, three-bathroom house so there is plenty of room and privacy for everyone.

We make the move and settle into the dynamics of a blended family. As much as I love the house I've raised the boys in for most of their young lives, I think this move gives us all the fresh start we need. There are no bad memories in our new place, a welcome change.

It isn't long before Justin finds a job and starts to get in a routine. His eating, exercise, and work habits are impressive; he is diving right back into life. He doesn't want to live with us; this was a short-term solution, and he is more than grateful that we were willing to give him the time he needs to start over. He is ready to get on with his life, and I am ready for him to do so as well. We have enjoyed some good moments; Justin is open and shares his newfound love for the Lord. He seems like the old Justin—only better; stronger and wiser.

And then my mom dies. This strong, woman of eighty-nine years took her last breath on February 9, 2014. She was my rock, my confidant, my friend, and my support. She was the backbone of our family—full of wisdom, and unconditional love. She supported me through Justin's journey and never gave up on him; he was special to her, and somehow, she always knew he would pull through his addiction. My mom had lost her husband and her youngest son, so she knew what suffering was, and she helped me stay the course. I pulled strength from her, and to think of living without her tore my heart wide open.

Shay sings "Amazing Grace" at the funeral, and both Dillon and Justin speak. It is a beautiful testimony of their love for my mom. Their Grandma was a huge part of their lives, and we will all miss her terribly. Justin speaks of having an angel to watch over him now that his grandma is with Jesus in heaven, and I believe he is right. My mom will be watching over us from above, and that gives me comfort. I feel grateful that Justin was healthy and thriving when Mom passed, and I know that she left this world with peace in her heart.

Then comes the engagement. Darwin asks my sons for their permission to have my hand in marriage, and they eagerly give their blessings. They love him and know how happy he makes me and are thrilled that we would finally be making it official. Darwin has me get my passport and request vacation time so I can go with him on a business trip to Paris. I have never traveled out of the country, so I am really looking forward to this adventure with him. With the ugliness behind me, I feel like it is time to start living again, so when he proposes to me on bended knee at the Eiffel tower, there is no hesitation in my "yessss." I burst into tears and my heart overflows with love for this beautiful man. Our wedding is scheduled for a year later. It is a glorious time for our family, and we are all looking forward to the future with the promise of good days ahead.

Justin looks great, his body muscular, his eyes bright. Soon he meets a girl that quickly becomes his girlfriend. She is a few years younger than he is and has just graduated from high school. She is a beauty, strikingly beautiful. I remember thinking it is not a good idea for him to be in a relationship at this point in his recovery, but he is an adult and must make his own decisions.

Then he starts drinking. As soon as I find out, I talk to him about it, and his response is that drinking was never his "thing," and that he was fine. I am furious. I got concerned earlier when he started drinking energy drinks again, so you can imagine my reaction when he told me he thought alcohol was okay. My confidence in him is starting to weaken. When Justin came home from Teen Challenge, I decided that I would do my best to trust him until he gave me a reason not to, and it was around this time that he gave me lots of reasons not to.

First it was drinking, then I noticed he was chewing tobacco again, and then the fights started. He was fighting a lot, typically over his girlfriend. Justin has a past that keeps coming back to haunt him. There is a lot of drama, and often it ends with fists flying. It isn't her fault, but her looks bring a lot of unwelcomed attention, and Justin finds himself in conflict almost every time they go out together. He is aggressive, and his fuse is getting shorter. The peace and contentment I sensed in him when he first came home has vanished.

He went through a few jobs, but finally landed a decent one with a local company. The pay is good, and they provide benefits; the only drawback is that it is the graveyard shift. The most recent fight broke a bone in his right hand, and since he is doing warehouse work, this poses a problem. I remember talking to him about it, and he admitted to me that he got some Vicodin® from a co-worker, and that was how he was able to work through the pain. He assures me that it was a "one-time" thing, and wasn't to fill a need or urge, but simply to dull the pain in his hand. I listen to his rationalization of using the same pills that just over four years ago had started this whole nightmare, and I go numb. I feel the color drain from my face, and my mouth is dry. I take deep breaths, trying hard not to completely lose it, and just watch him as he talks. When I can, I manage to get some words out, but they're coming out wrong. I can't think of what to say to my son who is heading down a dangerous path once again. I mutter a few warnings, and he responds thoughtfully; agreeing that he needs to check himself and straighten up. He seems sincere and as upset as I am, I am also grateful that he is being honest with me. He didn't have to tell me about the Vicodin, but he did. I know this is a setback, but I am not sure how bad it is. Somehow, I make it through the conversation and then quickly go up to my room, shutting the door behind me. I barely make it to the bathroom in time to throw up. My head is pounding. I lean against the doorway, wiping my face with a cold rag and pray to God that Justin will get back on track before it's too late.

One evening about a month later, we are having a family dinner. Everyone is seated around the table passing bowls of food, each involved in a different conversation with a steady noise of chatter humming in the air. I am not in the best mood, but I sit there trying to enjoy my dinner, when my eyes land on Justin who is sitting directly across from me. I slowly scan his face and upper body, his coloring, his eyes, and I lose my appetite completely. I put my fork down and sit quietly until everyone is done and has left the table. After cleaning up the dinner dishes, I catch Dillon as he is leaving the house and ask him, "Is it just me or does your brother look bad?" Dillon seems to reflect for a few seconds and responds, "Actually Mom, he looks just like I did when I worked the night shift. You have no life; you never see the sunshine, and you sleep all day. It's pretty miserable." I consider this for a moment and want to believe it, but I don't.

The next weekend, Justin goes to spend the night with my sister, and I grill her on the phone.

"Does he seem off to you?" I ask. There is a long pause.

"Well, I think he's tired, if that's what you mean. Don't worry about it; he'll be fine." In hindsight, I knew he was crashing, but I was grasping for hope; wanting to believe I was wrong.

Then Justin starts to spiral out of control. Again. He loses his job because he can't work with his hand hurt, his girlfriend is wondering why he looks so bad, and then things start disappearing around the house. One evening as he's pulling into the driveway, I walk out to confront him about money that is missing from our bedroom. He gives me the same response he used to give me when he was deep in his addiction; over dramatic shock and horror at the accusation. As I'm confronting him, I glance in the car, which is filthy. Out of habit, I grab the driver's side floor mat to shake off the dirt, and underneath there is a stash of pills.

As I start collecting his drugs, he tries to get around me, and I slam the door on his finger, crushing it. He looks at me wide-eyed and screams that his finger is broken. I ignore his tantrum, run into the house, and flush his stash down the toilet. He yells a warning that it's "not a good idea," because he was planning on detoxing himself at home. *Well, well, here we go again.* I tell him he's got to go. It's a terrible scene. Darwin has never witnessed me this angry, and I hate it. I just can't believe we're here again. I'm afraid my head will explode.

Justin admits his relapse, and we get him on a bus back to Teen Challenge in San Diego. He arrives but they won't take him. He's dope sick and hurting, but we manage to get him on another bus that takes him to Teen Challenge in Bakersfield. He spends Christmas detoxing and the next two weeks getting his head together. Then he calls, saying he's sorry, that he has gotten what he needs, and he's ready to come back home. It is a bump in the road; he's back on track.

He comes back home, apologizes, and takes responsibility for his relapse; we all try to get on with life. It lasts about two weeks before I notice things are missing again, and I don't have it in me to continue. I can't go another round, there won't be anymore "one more" times; he needs to leave.

A friend in recovery offers to let him live with him, and I warn the friend. "You know he's struggling, right? I'm kicking him out of our house, are you sure you want him in yours?" Jake, a big, gentle young man, assures me he knows what he's getting into. They pack up his bed and personal items and move Justin into his house, which is about fifteen miles from ours.

I meet Justin a few times and buy him groceries. He looks better but I'm guessing this new housing situation is not going to last long.

After about a month, Justin calls and tells me he can no longer live there because the owner of the house is moving back in. An hour later I get a call from Jake who says that Justin stole from him, and that he's back in his addiction. He goes on to explain that he made up a story to get Justin out of the house so they could change the locks.

I am shocked by how quickly he has fallen and feel sick when I think about what might happen next. I really thought he was going to make it this time, and I wonder if this nightmare will go on forever. I immediately call a locksmith to change our locks, and notify the alarm company to activate the alarm. I'm at the end of my rope with Justin; he will not live with us again.

They say that addicts need to hit "rock bottom" before recovery, and I wonder what rock bottom looks like for Justin. What could be worse than what we've already been through?

The locksmith arrives and asks if I'm having security problems. I tell him, "Yes, my son is a drug addict, and I don't want him here." My words come out before I can even think about what I'm saying, my voice doesn't sound like my own. The locksmith looks at me kindly and in a soft voice tells me he understands and will secure the house in no time.

I sit on the stairs and watch as he makes his way to each exterior door, and I think about the locks. I'm locking Justin out of our house and trying to build walls around my world so he can't get in. I'm trying to protect my family like I always have, except this time Justin is on the outside. I can't protect him anymore.

DRYER SHEETS

CHAPTER
THIRTEEN

KATHRYN

Justin checks in frequently and keeps me posted on what he's doing and the progress he's making. He's living in Folsom, which is about one and a half hours from Modesto. This is a comfortable distance for me; close enough that I can get to him if there's an emergency and far enough that I won't run into him anywhere. With all that we've been through, there needs to be distance between us.

Justin is staying at a shelter and working through his recovery, and he landed a job! He got hired at In-N-Out Burger and is two weeks into their six-week training program. I'm shocked that he was able to do well in an interview and so grateful they are giving him a chance. When he's clean, Justin can work circles around anybody, and I hope that he really is clean. Having been through so many rehabs and relapses, I don't have much confidence in him. I realize there's a slim chance that this latest plan of his will work, but I know I've done all I can do. I hold onto hope and try to believe in him. This is his life, it's his addiction, and he's got to figure it out. I love him, and I'm rooting for him, but it's from a distance. I cannot be a part of this life he's living or be around him when he's using, but I will not give up on him.

It's early on a Saturday, around 3:00 a.m., and I'm wide awake, so I take my phone and book and head downstairs. I turn the coffee on, pick up a throw blanket, and settle onto the couch. Even though I don't get enough sleep, I treasure the early morning hours. I love the quiet time before the sun rises and the stirring of the day begins.

As I'm waiting for my coffee to brew, I check the weather on my phone. I browse the morning news and get caught up on social media. I scroll through Facebook and see Justin's name tagged in a photo. My heart jumps immediately. There are three black and white pictures of Justin; he's shirtless, and he looks out of it. The post is by a girl I don't recognize and the caption says he is in her hotel room. Based on the comments, the photo implies that Justin is "good looking" or a "beautiful soul" but all I see is gray. There is nothing good about how he looks. I see that the post was made around midnight and the location shows Modesto, California. I feel the blood draining from my face and the pounding of my heart all the way up to my temples. *No, no, no, no, no!!! This cannot be happening. I just talked to Justin yesterday morning. He told me he's in Folsom, and he mentioned how great the training is going. He said he would have enough money in a month to rent a room.* We just had this conversation yesterday! I tell myself to just keep breathing, as the realization hits me. He was lying. He's in Modesto. There is no job at In-N-Out Burger; there is no plan; there is no progress; he hasn't been in Folsom, and he's using. I am going to lose it. Here I am again, blindsided by Justin. Why do I continue to fall for his lies?

After the initial shock wears off, I am angry to the point of, well, I don't know how to describe it, but it is bad. I private message the girl that posted the photos and tell her to take them down immediately. It is not a nice message, something like "I don't know who you are or what you think you're doing, but that is my son, and you need to take those pictures down right now!" I think about what to do next and remember that Justin still has my car and realize that this is a huge liability for me. He's in his addiction and probably using daily. I decide that I'm getting my car back *today*.

Justin still has a phone, so I try calling him nonstop for fifteen minutes, but he doesn't answer. I'm thinking, *once again you have turned my life completely upside-down Justin, and I'm not going to deal with this alone; you're going to feel every part of this chaos with me.* He finally answers, "What, Mom?" I tell him I'm taking my car back today. He starts to argue with me, and I cut him off. I respond slowly, my words deliberate and pronounced "We WILL meet today, and I WILL get my car from you, and if for some reason that doesn't happen then I'm calling the police." I add with sarcasm, "By the way, nice pictures on Facebook, Justin, and how's the job going in Folsom?" There is silence, and then he asks what pictures I'm talking about. He's high; I can hear it in his voice. I hang up because I can't stand it, and then I instantly have to fight the urge to call him right back and scream into the phone.

I look around trying to figure out what to do next and decide to start with the coffee I forgot about. I pour a cup, take a sip, and it's cold. Of course, it is. I fling the cup into the sink as hard as I can and hear it shatter, landing in a mess in my neat-as-a-pin kitchen. I don't bother cleaning it. I just stare at it and try to manage the anger that is now pounding like a jack hammer through my entire body.

I take a steaming hot shower hoping it will calm my nerves, but it doesn't help. I keep telling myself to get my car back and then I will be done with him. I just need my car, and then I'll be able to think clearly. About thirty minutes later, I check Facebook, and see that the pictures have been deleted so that tells me he's probably still with her, and now he knows that I know the truth about where and how he's living; that there is no job and that he's been lying about everything.

I call him back, and he immediately starts apologizing and making up excuses. I tell him I don't want to hear anymore; I just want my car. We plan to meet at three o'clock at the Burger King closest to our house. I wonder if he will show up. In my head I'm already rehearsing what I will say to the police.

Time seems to be moving in slow motion when Dillon walks through the door; I immediately ask if he'll come with me. I'm fairly certain that Justin is with Eric, and I don't want to deal with that alone. I just need to get my car back, that's all I want! Eric is a known drug user. A few years back, he went to school and played football with Dillon. I really like Eric, or I should say I like the clean and sober Eric. Back in high school, Eric and Dillon were friends and would sometimes hang out together. Eric was a good athlete and a nice looking, respectful young man. It wasn't until after graduation and the passing of his mother that Eric got lost in addiction, and, as far as I know, he's been into drugs ever since. Last I heard he was using heavily, and he and Justin started hanging out.

Dillon asks if everything is okay, and I tell him no, *nothing* is okay and explain what's going on. Dillon doesn't say anything, which irritates me for some reason. I guess I expected some kind of reaction. I can tell that the last thing he wants to do is get between me and his brother, but he agrees to come with me; feeling some obligation to make sure nothing bad happens.

I get through the day the best I can, but I'm in a state of high anxiety, and the anger just keeps building. It's two-thirty when I tell Dillon it's time to go; he responds, "It takes ten minutes to get there, Mom, just calm down. We will leave soon." I want to snap at him, but I don't. I just sit and wait.

Fifteen minutes later Dillon and I get in the car, and I'm driving fast. Dillon tells me to calm down and slow down, and I try to do both. We're three minutes into the drive when he demands I pull over so he can drive. By the tone in his voice, he is not asking me, he's telling me, so I concede and feel relief to sit in the passenger seat. We pull in the Burger King parking lot, and I see my car, a white Montero Sport I've owned for twelve years. Justin and Eric are standing beside it, and they're actually smiling. They look as if they are ready to greet us for a pleasant reunion of some sort. I'm thinking to myself, ohhhh man, this is not going to be good. I'm so wound up; I'm having a hard time staying in my seat. I look them over as we get closer; they both look like hell with their empty eyes and hollow faces. Before Dillon can even stop the car, I jump out and am walking, almost running over to them. Justin immediately puts his hands up, "Whoa, Mom, calm down, what's your problem?" and that was it for me.

"What's my problem, Justin? What's your freaking problem. What are you looking at, Eric?" Eric seems nervous; probably because Dillon is here, and I'm sure he's somewhat afraid of what Dillon might do.

Dillon is trying to approach the situation as a levelheaded person which in hindsight would have been a fantastic approach for me to consider as well, but I was beyond any logical thinking.

You know the term "temporary insanity"? It means you're

considered "insane" during an act or crime, and then after it's over, you return to being "sane." That is the best way to describe me at that point. People that have "temporary insanity" do things they wouldn't normally do. Like, for instance, hurt or kill people. Obviously, I did not physically hurt or kill anyone, but I was out of my mind.

I scream at Justin to give me the keys, and he tosses them in my direction, acting like he's afraid to get too close to me. His reactions just fuel my anger more. I start opening all the doors to my car inspecting it, and it is filthy. Justin watches and tells me, "Oh sorry Mom, I was gonna clean it for you, but I didn't get a chance." I stop and look at him.

"What? You didn't get a chance, Justin? Because you're too busy screwing up your life? Is that it? Too busy getting high?" My voice is getting louder. At this point I'm throwing things out of the car with the three boys just standing back and watching me. I see the grime and dirt build up, the window that is broken, the torn seat covers, and I am disgusted. I push Justin with both my hands on his chest when Eric starts to say something, I scream and call him a "junkie" and tell him to back off. At this point we are causing quite a scene. Dillon is pulling me back, doing his best to get me to the car. People are walking by and looking at us. Eric is looking down; Justin and I are wide-eyed, and it's a frenzy. It feels like a scene out of movie. I don't even feel like I'm in my own body; it's like I'm watching this from somewhere else, because I can't believe it's really happening. We don't yell in our family; we don't cuss, and we don't act like this, but here we are.

Dillon and I have to drive home separately because now we have two cars. Dillon's busy getting the guys to leave and trying to get me back to the car so we can get out of there, but before I get in the driver's seat, I pop the trunk and look in the back and see more junk. I throw the blankets and pillow on the ground when I notice an opened box of dryer sheets and a few sheets scattered throughout the car. I realize that the entire time I was going through the car that has been completely trashed, I kept wondering why it didn't smell bad and smelled sort of fresh. I recognize this was Justin's attempt to get rid of the ugly drug smell that had saturated the car; in preparation of giving it back to me. This gives me pause; *He's trying to make the car smell good, so I don't see the filth?* I don't know why I am so tripped out by this, but I am. *Justin, you're literally lying to me about everything in your life, you're probably shooting heroin into your body every single day, and yet, you take the time to buy, or probably steal, dryer sheets so I don't get mad that my car stinks?*

I cover my face in my hands and try to pull myself together, shaking from the adrenaline. Dillon walks up slowly, as if approaching a spooked animal, and for what seems like the tenth time tells me to calm down and asks if I can drive home. I nod, get in the driver's seat, start the car, and burn rubber out of the parking lot.

Pulling up to the house, I'm rattled by what just happened, but feeling justified in my actions. I'm still furious. I grab a bottle of water out of the refrigerator and sit on the couch trying to take deep breaths, as I can still feel my heart pounding in my chest. I hear the garage door open, and Dillon walks in and lets me have it. "What is wrong with you? What the hell was that? You act like a maverick with no regard for anyone or anything; you just bulldozed your way in and made everything so much worse! What is wrong with you?" Dillon *never* yells at me; he can be hard to get along with sometimes, but he never yells. He grabs his keys and slams the door on his way out.

I sit there and stare at the door he just slammed and try to understand what just happened. I'm mad at him too; how dare he call me out when I haven't caused any of this. I have had it with *everything.* I sit there with my head in my hands trying to pull myself together, and then remember the filthy car sitting in my driveway and spend the next two hours cleaning it inside and out, trying to erase every bit of the dark, grungy life Justin is living. As I'm cleaning under the seats, I find a hypodermic needle. I sit back, lean against the car door and stare at it for a few minutes. I take a deep breath and think to myself, well, there it is, the ultimate ending to this horrible day, the final slap in the face from Justin. At this point, I have every cleaning supply from the house out in the driveway, including a toothbrush for the hard to get to spots. I clean and clean until I finally give in to the exhaustion. I walk slowly back into the house, physically and emotionally spent. The house is empty and oddly quiet. I take a shower, skip dinner, and go to my bedroom even though it's only eight o'clock at night.

I'm mad at EVERYTHING; my coffee for being cold, the drugs that have stolen my son, that hypodermic needle that seemed to taunt me, and I hate that stupid car that I don't even want anymore. I wonder how our family has landed in this miserable place. My energy is zapped, and I fall asleep quickly.

I wake up at 4:00 a.m. in an instant panic. I turn on the light and collect myself as my mind settles on what day it is, the time, and then the memories of yesterday come flooding in—it hits me hard.

Have you ever heard a story about someone really making a fool of themselves and wondered how awful that must feel? For example, it's the company holiday party and you're in a high-level position. You get drunk and do some things that are inappropriate. You flirt with a coworker, or you fall on the dance floor, or you start an argument with someone, spill your drink on your boss, or whatever. Now you're at home but can't remember how you got there. The sun rises, and you wake up and look at the clock realizing you're already late for work. As the fog in your head clears, you start to remember the events from the night before, and you are mortified. Shame starts creeping in, and you wonder how you will face everyone. People cannot "un-see" what you did; it can't be erased, because it happened, and people witnessed it. Now you must face it. You just want to crawl into a hole and never come out.

That sums up how I feel after waking up this morning. What did I do? What is wrong with me? I think about what Dillon said, and he was right. I'm so embarrassed. I was completely out of control. From the moment I saw the Facebook post, I totally lost it.

Justin has done some terrible things in his addiction, but why can't I be gentle and love him through it? I remember watching a documentary about a Fresno State star athlete that turned into a raging addict; it was heartbreaking to watch what he went through and what he became. In the documentary, his dad was interviewed, and in the kindest and gentlest way, he talked about his son being lost and that he just waited until he was better; meeting him where he was, loving him and having faith that he would get through it, and he did get through it; he finally beat his addiction and made a life for himself. There was no sign of rage or anger, not a trace of it in this dad. Just patience, love, and tolerance. Why can't I be like that dad? My God, why can't I just love Justin through it?

I feel like I went back to the thirteen-year-old girl that would smash my parent's vodka bottle on the kitchen floor, hoping it made them feel bad when they saw it the next morning. Or when I came home to a messy house with mom and dad already tipsy, so I open every cupboard in our hallway and kick them shut, one after another as hard as I could, just taunting them to say something to me—but they never would. A switch flipped in me yesterday, and I lost control.

If I'm being completely honest, I think I wanted to hurt Justin somehow. I wanted to scream at him and hit him until he snaps out of this darkness, so he would remember who he is. Why can't he stop? My heart starts racing again, and I recognize that this is where the anger is coming from. I don't understand how he got in this awful place, I don't understand the terrible things he's doing, and all the lies, and I don't understand when he became so weak. I hate addiction. I HATE ADDICTION!

Life goes on, Justin is doing whatever Justin does when he's homeless and on drugs and as much as I want to call him, apologize, and tell him I love him, I just can't bring myself to do it. I know he's with Eric and heard they left town which brings on new pangs of worry.

Dillon and I have been silent for two days. I need to apologize and take responsibility, but I dread even mentioning it. I vow to never, no matter what is happening, never allow myself to get to that place of madness again.

I can't seem to stop thinking about that day and can't believe I called Eric a junkie. It's not at all funny, but I laugh because I didn't say it to Justin. Am I that prideful and delusional that I'm still holding Justin in a separate category, somehow in better standing? Wow, I am so broken and confused. I need to get it together.

I think about this dark place that Justin has taken residence in. I know he would never have chosen it, and I also know that his choices keep him a prisoner there. But he is not doing this *to me.* I have never doubted how much Justin loves me, but this has nothing to do with me or the love between us. He isn't intentionally trying to destroy me; he needs to figure this out, but this shouldn't be a battle between us. Justin has his hands full with these demons that have a grip on him, and I need to bow out of the fight.

I finally apologize to Dillon, a quick apology with not a lot of detail. He doesn't look at me but gives me a nod, and that's the last we speak of it. I make dinner as a silent peace offering, and he eats, so that's a good sign.

I decide I need two things; go to the track and call my sister. I do both, and it does help. Running the bleachers feels good, and releases my nervous energy. When I call Martha, I explain, in gory detail, all that happened and her response is, "Well, it's not like you killed someone. Don't worry about it; it's fine." She always knows what to say; her response makes me feel better. I am so thankful for my sister.

I'm going to try and forget that day ever happened, and I'm going to do better. For the love of God, *I must do better.*

JUSTIN

We're in a hotel room in Modesto, and I'm in a comfortable haze. My phone has been dead for hours, but I finally have a charger, so I plug it into the wall. I hear it buzzing and ignore it. Whatever it is, it can wait. I nod off.

The girl that is letting me stay with her is hitting me on the arm.

"Hey, your phone keeps buzzing, it's been buzzing for a long time, answer it!"

I open my eyes and try to gather my thoughts. I look around the dark room and see garbage strewn everywhere, and people sleeping on the floor. I wonder who they are and how long I've been here.

I look at the clock, and it's not even 5:00 a.m. *Who would be calling?* I check my phone and have twelve missed calls from my mom. That's bad. What could it be now? I'm out of her house, and she thinks I'm in Folsom working and doing well, because that's what she wants to believe. I've become good at telling mom what she wants to hear. She just wants to know that I'm making progress, I'm gaining weight and that I'm clean, and even though none of those things are true, that's what I tell her.

I don't feel like dealing with her right now, but she keeps calling. I have to call her back, but I need to give myself a little time to come down; I'm too high to talk. Before I can finish that thought, my phone starts buzzing again.

"Mom, what?" Her voice is low and strained. She tells me she's taking her car back today. I try to think of what to say, but she catches me off guard by asking about pictures of me on Facebook and how the job in Folsom is going. I have no response—there's dead silence on the phone. I'm not sure what to say, but this isn't good. I need that car; it's my only place to sleep. I try to convince her, but she is not buying it; she's threatening to call the cops and I know she'll do it. She hangs up on me.

This girl put pictures of me on Facebook. Are you kidding? No, no, no, noooooo! I tell her to take them down, and she does. My mom messaged her something crappy, and she's complaining about it, but I could not care less. I don't even really know her. I try to think; now my mom knows I'm in Modesto, and that I've been lying about everything. This is not good. I'm just trying to survive, and I do not want to deal with this. I wish she would just back off. I try to prepare myself, because I know she's going to call back, but I just can't think right now. She does call back, and I try my best to apologize and make it right with her, but it doesn't work. I'm desperate to keep this car, but she won't even give me a chance. This car is the only way I can hustle money, it's what I use to steal, to sleep, to get dope, and to see my girlfriend who happens to also believe that I'm working in Folsom. I am so screwed.

We set a time to meet so she can have her precious car. I need to be there on time. I don't want the cops looking for me, and I know she's at the point that she'll call them. I'm hoping when we meet, I can talk her out of it, but we'll see; I never know how she's going to react.

I tell Eric we need to meet my mom at three o'clock and to make sure I'm awake at two-thirty so I can take a shower first. He wakes me; I shower and try to pull myself together. We head out, and as we're walking, we pass a laundromat. I see a box of dryer sheets on the counter by someone's clothes—I grab it and stuff it in my jacket. I'll throw them in the car, so it smells good, because she's gonna freak out that her car isn't clean. Me and Eric throw out the trash in the car and try to clean it up as best we can. We barely have enough gas in the tank to get there, but we make it. I really hope I look okay and that this goes well. I do not want to lose this car.

We drive to Burger King, and wait. I check myself in the side mirror. I look okay, except I'm pale. I slap my face, trying to get some color back in it.

I spot Mom's car pulling in, and Dillon is driving. Oh no, this is not good. I did not expect him here. Eric is nervous, and I am too. I try to smile so I look normal, but as soon as I see Mom, I know she's done with me. She practically jumps out of the car and is looking at me with disgust. My heart is racing; I just want her to calm down and listen to me, but she won't; she's acting psycho.

I can't get a word in, and at this point I just wish she'd take the keys and go. She's yelling at Eric and calling him names and acts like she hates my guts. Well, I hate you too! I just want to scream at her, *I hate you too, Mom!* She keeps coming at me; she even pushes me. I don't think I've ever seen her this mad. I try to react in a way that makes her feel sorry for me somehow, but that doesn't even work. My hands are up. Do your thing, Mom. Take your piece of crap car; I don't care anymore.

Dillon is trying to manage, but I can tell he's mad too. He tells me and Eric to leave, so I guess the car is gone. We take off walking and decide to get out of Modesto. Things are going bad here anyway. People are looking for us; my girlfriend is done with me, but she keeps calling. The police are on my back; detectives are calling; I have no home, no car, no money, and my family wants nothing to do with me. That means I have nothing left to lose. Nothing.

Eric is on the phone with our dealer trying to find a place to meet before we get a ride to the Bay Area. We sit on the curb, and I try to gather my thoughts. Am I beyond hope? Should I ask God to breathe life and light back into me? The darkness promises quick relief to the pain; it moves through my body like a black serpent that slithers through my veins, and I can't resist it. Have I fallen too far from His grace? I think about the darkness. I picture it like a seductive lover, pulling me in, caressing every ache and hurt inside and slowly, methodically trying to destroy me. How did I fall so far again? I was clean for almost two years.

We walk to the park and meet our dealer and use the rest of our money to get a bag of dope. We sit behind some bushes, and I watch

Eric inject the dark liquid; his eyes become heavy, as the warmth hits him. I take my turn and let the warmth fill me too. It moves to each and every part of my body, and I have instant relief from all my pain. We will make it; we will get out of this town, and I will leave behind all these problems and people that seem to matter less and less.

Eric's friend agrees to give us a ride, so I crawl into the back of his car, and we head to the Bay Area. I feel the warmth hit every nerve and muscle in my frail body, and I feel good again. I have nothing left to lose. There's no one that I have to answer to. I have nothing but this warmth that keeps me floating, so I will leave all that is familiar and good. I'm not going to resist any longer, because I don't care anymore. I just wanna plunge into the darkness and let it swallow me.

"BE STILL, AND KNOW
THAT I AM GOD!"

Psalm 46:10

BLUE EYES

CHAPTER
FOURTEEN

KATHRYN

I thought I would feel relief having the locks changed and Justin out of the house, but it didn't bring the kind of relief I was hoping for. Turns out you can't erase someone out of your life, not when you love them so much that it actually hurts your heart. I carry the burden of Justin's addiction around with me like a heavy backpack that I cannot take off. I feel captive to it somehow; like it's suffocating me. Most of the time I manage it, but some days I just can't. I never know what's going to happen next, and I'm not sure where Justin is or what he's doing, but I do know he's using.

I try to keep the same schedule and find satisfaction in routine. I get up at 5:00 a.m. and drink my coffee, read the morning devotional, check emails, and prepare for my day. I shower and get ready for work, put gym clothes in my bag and usually arrive to work by 7:30 in the morning. I like to get there before others, so I have time to sit in my office and collect my thoughts before the hustle of the day begins. I throw myself into my work, usually eating at my desk for lunch, and finish my day around 5:30 p.m., workout, come home, shower, eat dinner with Darwin, watch a little TV, and then do it all over again the next day. On weekends, I clean house, catch up on laundry, hang out, watch movies, and prep our meals for the coming week. I grocery shop, wash the cars, check-in with my sister; just regular life stuff. I keep busy and try to avoid any social gatherings as much as I can, because I don't really want to talk to anyone.

I'm feeling extra anxious one morning as I'm driving to work. I didn't sleep well the night before and I'm not prepared for the long day of meetings that lie ahead of me. I pull up to a stop light and glance to my right and see a young man, probably Justin's age, sitting on a bus bench. He is barefoot and wearing a baggy t-shirt and a pair of shorts that hang on his bony hip bones. It's probably forty degrees outside, and he is shivering. He is obviously homeless and in need. He has long red hair that looks like it hasn't been washed or combed in weeks, and he has blue eyes as bright and beautiful as the morning sky. Even in his disheveled state, you can't help but notice his eyes. He looks like a dirty, scared, little boy to me, so I roll down the passenger window, lean over and ask him if he's okay. He stands and walks over to my car and says he's alright, just down on his luck and struggling with some things. I feel a pull to try and help him, so I hand him a shawl that's in the backseat of my car. He quickly wraps it around his shoulders and thanks me. The light turns green, but I stay and keep talking to him. I give him a bottle of water and the five dollars I have in my wallet. I tell him that the shawl belonged to my mom, and that she passed away just a year ago.

"Please make sure to take care of it."

His eyes widen. He takes off the shawl and hands it back to me. "I can't take this from you; it just doesn't seem right."

I tell him to keep it and to take care of himself. He thanks me and goes back to the bench. The person behind me honks, so I roll up the window and drive off and wonder if it is drugs or mental illness that has brought him to the streets. I wonder if he has a mom and dad out there that are worried about him. I think about my mom's shawl that I treasured and wonder if I made a mistake by giving it to him. I cry for the rest of my drive to work.

I get through my meetings and tasks for the day, but I am not focused. I have a hard time caring about my "to do list" and the unfinished work sitting in front of me, knowing that Justin is out there somewhere doing God knows what. Most days I can keep Justin tucked away out of my thoughts so I can focus on other things, but not today. I keep thinking of Justin and the boy at the bus stop. I hope the young man will find his way, and I wonder if people drive by my son thinking the same thing.

Around three-thirty in the afternoon, I feel like I cannot sit in my office for one more minute. I clean off my desk, wipe down my shelves, prepare my work for the next day, and grab my stuff. I let my boss and team members know I am leaving for the day.

Five minutes into the drive home, I stop on the side of the road, think for a minute, and make a U-turn. I need to do something. I need to talk to someone. I feel overwhelmed with sadness, and I cannot go home yet. I say a prayer, and before I know it, I'm driving to a local church that I have attended a few times. I park my car and walk in, following the signs to the administration office. An older woman with a soft voice sits behind the reception desk, and asks if she can help me. I tell her I need to talk to someone. She asks if I have an appointment.

"No, do I need one? I'm sorry to barge in here like this, but I'm really struggling. I got in my car and drove here hoping someone could talk to me." My voice is shaky, and I am fighting back tears; I think she senses how upset I am.

She reaches over and grips my hand in hers, looks me in the eyes, and says with confidence, "You sit here for just a minute, my dear, and let me see who I can find for you to talk to. I will be right back, okay?"

I try to smile, thank her, and say I will wait. She is sweet and makes me miss my mom. I think about the shawl again and wonder what the blue-eyed boy is doing. The tears are already starting, but I am fighting them. I'm not sure why I came here or what I will say if someone actually comes to talk to me, but I don't leave; I just stare at the floor, hold my breath, and wait.

About ten minutes later, a man walks in and asks if he can help me. I tell him I need to talk to someone in private. The lady with the soft voice comes quickly around the corner and introduces the man as Jason, and tells me that he will help me. She is out of breath, and I get the feeling that she has worked hard to find someone for me to talk to. She gives me a wink; her kindness makes me want to cry even more. Jason points me to an office off the hallway and tells me to take a seat in the chair next to the window, and he sits in front of a small desk. Jason apologies for making me wait; he explains that normally they would have a woman speak with me but there is no one available so I am stuck with him. I smile at his joke and appreciate what I think is his attempt to make me feel more comfortable. He offers me a water, which I take, and then he asks how he can help me. There's a ringing in my ears and I'm having a hard time figuring out where to start; I have no idea what to say and I can't remember why I even came here. Jason tells me to take all the time I need.

I close my eyes for a moment and dig deep for the strength I need to have this conversation. I blurt out, "It's my son. He's an addict, and he's on the street and I can't, I just can't, I don't know what to do, I just...." And I start sobbing. He hands me tissue and sits quietly as I cry and let the held-back tears flow. After a few minutes, I take a deep breath, wipe my eyes, and apologize for the outburst. "It's been a rough day, and I just can't seem to get it together." He smiles, tells me it's fine, and asks if he can start our talk with a prayer. He puts his hand on my shoulder and says a prayer, asking God to wrap his arms around me and to bring comfort to this mother who is hurting for her child. His prayer goes straight to my heart.

We both sit back down, and he asks me to continue. With the tears shed, I decide I've got nothing to lose, and I tell him about Justin and his history of addiction. I talk about how he relapsed after being sober for almost two years, and pull no punches with the severity of Justin's situation. I think I see a smile on his face, which confuses me. He must have picked up on my sudden discomfort, because he apologizes and says, "God is so good."

I'm thinking that it's an odd time to smile and tell me that God is good, especially when I'm pouring out my soul and have been crying for the last ten minutes. Jason continues, "I know exactly why you ended up here today talking to me. I was the worst of the worst of addicts; I was a complete drug fiend." I look at him in shock and sit quietly, hoping he will keep talking so I don't have to, and he does. Jason continues and tells me his story, as I sit and listen in pure amazement. This guy has been through it all. He is in recovery from a long-term heroin addiction that caused him to lose everything. He's lost two wives with failed marriages because of addiction; he's lost numerous jobs, his home, money, and eventually had to move out of state. He overdosed twice, and it's a miracle that he's still alive. He credits a men's discipleship program called "The Mission House" in Washington state for saving his life. He's been clean for five years.

He asks if Justin knows the Lord, and I tell him yes, that he was saved when he was at Teen Challenge. Jason reacts, "Good; you need to find comfort in that; he has salvation through Jesus Christ, so we need to focus on you, how are you taking care of yourself?" This question surprises me. I want to say that I didn't come here to talk about me. I came to talk about Justin, but I don't say it; I just sit and listen. We continue to talk, and he encourages me to join a small group and to seek comfort in the Lord. I nod my head as if I'm agreeing with him, but I know that I'm not going to a group. There is no way I'm talking in a group about Justin, but I will seek the Lord. I don't know what to do next, but I sit there waiting for some kind of plan, and Jason has one. God bless him.

He hands me his business card and writes the website for The Mission House program on the back of it. He tells me to look at the website and to give Justin his phone number and tell him to call him. I feel the tension of this horrible day fall away and am so grateful I came to this church. Jason has given me something positive to think about, and his testimony gives me hope. As we get up and I'm about to leave, I thank him and tell him how much I appreciate his time. He smiles and reminds me it was God that summoned this meeting between us, not him. He encourages me to give Justin his number and says he is anxious to talk to him. He offers to be a support to me as well and says he will pray for us.

Jason is probably in his mid-thirties and has an easy way about him; I feel comfortable and am grateful for his support and I think I might keep in touch with him. He's walked in Justin's shoes and knows what the life of addiction is like. This guy can help me with Justin. I sit in my car for a few minutes and collect myself before I head home.

Darwin is out of town on business tonight, so I'll have the house to myself which is good; I don't feel like talking. I pull into the driveway and walk in the house. This big house that we rented for our family feels empty and cold tonight.

I throw my stuff down in the living room and look in the refrigerator, but nothing appeals to me. I pour a glass of my favorite white wine that Darwin left for me and go upstairs to our bedroom, leaving a trail of clothes on the stairs. I put on a pair of Darwin's boxers and an oversized t-shirt, wash my face, and put my hair up. I feel better. The sorrow that was suffocating me earlier today has retreated, and I can breathe again. I start to get in bed, and then instead, drop to my knees and pray, "Thank you, God, for letting me talk to Jason. Please Lord help me and Justin, please, please, please God, help us find our way, . . ." and then I pray for the blue-eyed boy at the bus stop, "God, please help him too." I get up from my knees and crawl in bed and try to read, but I can't focus on the words. I put the book down and think back to a conversation Justin and I had a few months back. We were arguing; I was accusing him of something, and he looked at me like he really hated me and said that he was sorry he couldn't be "perfect like me." I wonder if he really believes I expected him to be perfect. Before drugs, he was beautiful and everything I could have ever wanted in a son. Doesn't he recognize that?

I remember when he was in fourth grade and signed up to run in the school jog-a-thon. He spent weeks convincing family and friends to sponsor him and was thrilled that he could raise money for his school. He raised a total of one hundred dollars, which was a lot more than I thought he would collect. The night before the jog-a-thon, he went to bed extra early, had his clothes laid out, and his water jug filled up and in the refrigerator so it would be nice and cold. We talked about him getting a good night's sleep and agreed on what I would make him for breakfast in the morning before the big event. Eggs, toast, orange juice, and yogurt with granola was on the menu. He woke up and did some stretches, ate his breakfast, and combed his hair just right. I dropped him off at school with a promise to be back early enough to bring him his Gatorade before the jog-a-thon started.

It's one o'clock in the afternoon when I pull up to the school with his lime-flavored Gatorade as promised. I spot him warming up on the field. The other kids are gathered around giggling and having fun, but Justin is taking his warm-up seriously. When he saw me, a big grin crossed his face; he ran up and hugged me tight. He whispered, "Mom, wait until you see how fast I run, you're not even gonna believe it." I laughed and told him to relax and have fun, and assured him that I would be watching every single minute.

The jog-a-thon starts, and Justin is sprinting ahead of all the kids. I watch as he gains momentum and runs his little heart out. The other kids are taking an easy pace and having fun, but my son is determined to set some kind of record. He ran a gazillion laps, and finally the principal called the end of the jog-a-thon. Justin's face is red, and dripping with sweat. I'm guessing he ran more than all the other kids combined. He was happy with his performance and asked the coach how many laps he did, and I saw them give each other high fives. He was ecstatic with his victory. I hug him tightly and tell him I'll see him after I get off work.

We get home, and my phone rings. It's his after-school care teacher; she wanted to check on Justin and make sure he was feeling alright. I tell her he seemed fine and ask why she was concerned. She told me that after returning to the classroom, Justin vomited. When she asked him if he needed to go home, he said no, he was fine. She thought he just over did it at the jog-a-thon because it was so hot outside, but wanted to make sure he was okay. I thanked her, hung up the phone, and went to tuck Justin in and say goodnight. I told him how proud I was of him and that he did a good job, and asked if he was okay. He said he was fine and that he had the best time ever. I ask him about getting sick afterwards, and he rolls his eyes, "Oh my gosh, Mom, I'm fine, I just ran a lot more than everyone else, so I threw up, but it was soooo much fun!" His eyes were sparkling, and he fell fast asleep before I could turn off the light.

I remember thinking what a little bundle of energy he was; he couldn't seem to do anything in moderation. He was all in or not at all; that was my son. My sweet little boy with the big brown eyes ran like the wind today.

I tuck him in and watch him sleep for just a few minutes more, watching the steady rise and fall of his chest. His dark lashes sprayed along the top of his cheeks. His hair smelled like apples and spice, and was still wet from the shower. I turned his light out and instead of going to bed, I snuggled up with him for a few minutes. He didn't wake up, but he instinctively wrapped his hand around my arm and pulled it close to his chest, and we drifted off to sleep together.

The memory is comforting, but it makes me wonder why he

pushed himself so hard. Was there pressure to always succeed and do better than others? What drove him to such extremes? I don't have answers, just memories of a strong little boy that wanted to make his mark on the world.

I turn off the light and try to sleep but I can't. The clock reads 3:39 a.m. I wonder what the blue-eyed boy is doing and if he still has my mom's shawl.

"GOD CAN'T GIVE US PEACE AND
HAPPINESS APART FROM HIMSELF
BECAUSE THERE IS NO SUCH THING."

C.S. Lewis

CHAPTER

FIFTEEN

KATHRYN

I miss my mom. I miss her so much, and at the same time, I'm grateful that she's not here to see Justin's last relapse. I'm glad that when she left this world, she saw nothing but his beauty.

I think about my mom and dad and what a joy it was to watch them in their roles as Grandparents. When the kids were small, once a month we would visit them when they lived in Columbia, California, a charming Gold Rush town about an hour's drive from our house. They lived in a quaint, bright yellow house that sat in the middle of a quarter-acre lot on a quiet little highway. The fence around their house was lined with rose bushes and hydrangeas that seemed to always be in bloom. There were trees for climbing, and lots of lawn to run around on. I always liked to sit on their squeaky, old, rusted porch swing and drink iced tea as I watched my dad play with the kids. All the memories of my struggles as a young girl seemed to disappear as I watched my parents love my children; I really cherished our times together.

During the drive to their house, we would always pass a little white pony in his stable next to the road. As we drove up the rolling hills and rounded the corner, Justin would loudly exclaim, "I bet the pony is going to be around this corner!" Much to his delight, the little white pony would be standing in his corral, watching us. Justin would gasp and then giggle and wave to the pony as if it were the best thing he'd ever seen.

When we arrived at Grandma and Grandpa's, he would first tell Grandma about the pony and then run to Grandpa and ask, "Is it time to take the flag out?" Grandpa would answer with much enthusiasm, "Well, I don't know soldier, you haven't saluted me yet!" And just like that Justin, Dillon, and Shay would stand up straight, click their heels together and proudly salute. Grandpa would respond with an "About face! Hup two, three, four, hup, two, three four." I watched my little family line up behind my dad, marching with their heads held high, on to the front porch to put up the American Flag so it could wave gloriously throughout the day. Mom and I were both delighted with their little parade.

I smile at the memory and the purity of their love. Life seemed so simple and easy back then. My thoughts turn back to Justin. I just don't understand how, after almost two years clean, he can plunge right back into addiction. It's like he started in the shallow water dabbling in drugs; soon he moved into the deep end of the pool where he lost his footing and could not stand anymore, and now he's so deep underwater that he seems to have disappeared completely. I don't know how else to explain it. Justin is gone, and I don't know who this person is that has taken over his body.

Back when this all started, I was told that relapse is part of the recovery process, and it just doesn't make sense to me. I can understand that you find yourself in a situation where something gets a grip on you and before you know it, you're dependent, and that dependency, that physical and mental need and urge lands you in an ugly place of addiction. And then you figure it out; you seek treatment, you go through detox and a program or get therapy or do whatever you need to do, and now you're "informed." Maybe you relapse once, thinking you're above it somehow and will be fine, but you end up back in that same place of desperation. At this point, without a doubt, you know your temptations, your weaknesses, and what you need to stay away from. So how is relapse after relapse an expected and "normal" part of the recovery process? You've tried that path, and you know exactly where it's going to take you. Every single time, it strips you of everything good and leaves you empty and in despair, and yet, you still go back there, Justin. You just keep diving back in. I wonder what is so broken inside of you that you can't pull out of this.

I've watched documentaries and read books about drug addiction, and it seems like an evil romance. Drugs have destroyed your integrity, ruined your relationships, hurt the ones you love the most, and yet you still go back. I am so over this. At some point, Justin is making decisions that take him back to this dark, ugly place. I feel like he is choosing it; he has all the information he needs to make good decisions, and he keeps choosing the nightmare. I hate it with every ounce of my being.

After these last several months, I know that my part in this is over. If he wants to get help, when and if he is ever ready, then I will help him, but it won't include him living under the same roof with me, and I will no longer be a part of his chaos. You want to be a drug addict, Justin? Then go be one. Do your thing, buddy! Live that life to the fullest, do all the drugs you want, and I'll be over here waiting for the call that you've overdosed, and then I'll plan your funeral. That's where my head is at today.

Justin is living on the streets in the Bay Area with his drug buddy, Eric, the one I called a junkie. They hang out in a horrible, drug-infested part of town. I know this because I drove through there once and almost got carjacked. I was with Shay, driving around to see where Justin was living. We pulled up to a stop sign and were looking around, when this guy appeared out of nowhere, met eyes with me, and started running towards the car. Shay yelled at me to go, and we sped out of there, scared to death. Seriously, I wouldn't drive through there again, much less live there, but this is where Justin has taken up residence. These streets are now his home.

As I look back, I recognize that each relapse was worse than the previous one. Each time a little more intense and desperate, but now he's at an entirely different level. Justin has turned into a criminal, and in some ways, I feel like he's enjoying it. Now that everything is exposed and there are no more lies to tell, he is free. He's out of our home, out of our lives, and he can go do his thing without holding back. Without seeing the faces of the people he loves, he can freely pursue drugs. He doesn't have to hide anymore; there are no more secrets. I feel like there is some relief for him in that. I think he stays high most of the time because if he gets any clarity, if he even gets a glimpse of what he has become, I know it will destroy him. As long as he is high and numb, he doesn't have to think about us or face the reality of the life he is living.

The crazy part is that he still manages to find a way to keep in touch with me. I hear from him sometimes daily but at least several times a week, and I'm not exactly sure why he calls. The conversations are brief. He never asks me for anything, and that's how I know he's gotten good at criminal life. Most of the time when he calls, I can tell he's high. He'll tell me he's doing well, getting into detox, going into a program or getting a job soon. I just listen. He doesn't come back into town as far as I know. Since the locks have been changed, he hasn't been back to our home, but he still calls, so at least I know he's alive.

I'm not holding up very good through this. There are calluses that have formed around my heart and a numbness that has settled inside me. It's like all the feelings are worn out; expired somehow. Except for anxiety, I still have plenty of that. I'm relieved that he is out of town and that he doesn't include me in his chaos, but there is no peace. Sleep is hard to come by, but I still manage to work, keep my house in order, get my workouts in, and love my family, but there is a huge emptiness at the loss of my son. I am waiting to hear that he is dead; I mean, where else could this be leading?

I think about Justin dying a lot. I run it over in my mind like a movie; the phone ringing and an officer asking if I'm the parent of a "Justin Dean Usiak," Caucasian male, brown hollow eyes, brown hair, gray skin, twenty-two years old, 5'11" tall, approximately 160 pounds of emptiness, is that your son? I see myself falling to the ground and crying hysterically, or sometimes I see myself hanging up the phone and getting in my car and driving for the rest of my life, never stopping. I have visions of me hiding in my closet, so I don't have to face what's next. It's on my mind all the time; I can't seem to stop the thoughts or the visions that keep playing in my head.

I remember a Saturday afternoon getting a call from Justin. I hear his familiar "Hey, Mom" and we chat a little bit. He tells me he's still in Oakland and on a waiting list for a new program, he's eating and feeling pretty good, and so on. I interrupt.

"Justin, I need you to think about this. When you overdose and die, what kind of arrangements do you want?" It's quiet for a moment, and then he replies with a laugh.

"What are you talking about?"

"I need to know what you want. I won't be in any condition to make decisions, and I need to know how to handle it. Do you want an open casket or closed? Am I supposed to invite everyone or keep it private? Are there certain songs you want played? I need your help with this because I won't be able to manage it on my own."

Dead silence ensues, and then, "Mom, stop! Why are you doing this? Mom! What the hell?" ... and he hangs up.

I sit on the stairs in our house, holding the phone on my lap, and Dillon walks in; apparently, he overheard part of the conversation from the living room. He's looking at me with eyebrows raised, "Why would you do that, Mom? Why would you say that to him?" He doesn't wait for a response; he just walks away. I think about it, considering his words, and I don't regret the conversation. Justin calls me and talks as if somehow this life he's living is okay. Well, it's not okay. I don't think Justin can survive this way very much longer, and I don't know if he can get clean, so what else is there? At some point we're going to lose him if he doesn't figure it out, that is the reality.

I'm not sure why I always want Justin to feel my suffering, but I do; I want him to face this and feel every part of it, hoping it may shock him back to us. I want my son back.

I've taken the gloves off and bowed out of the fight, but others are still trying. I remember getting a phone call from Shay saying that Justin reached out to her. She met him and bought him some food. She said his skin was gray, and he's so thin that his cheek bones look sharp. She got him and Eric a hotel room for one night and then took them to the Salvation Army thrift store and bought them a tent and a suitcase with rollers so they would have a place to put their belongings. They were thankful for her help. She left them under a bridge somewhere while they were setting up camp for the night. I can hear the heartache in her voice and the pain of feeling helpless. I do my best to encourage her and tell her I'm grateful that she tried to help her brother. I love her so much for trying, and I know how much she loves Justin. I feel some relief that at least on this day I know he ate and had something to drink.

David, one of my lifelong friends that I consider family, gave it a try as well. David is from the Bay Area and has raised two sons of his own who have had their share of struggles. I love all three of them with my whole heart, and I am grateful for his efforts with Justin. They connected somehow, and David was supposed to meet Justin and Eric at the BART station when he walked right past them, not recognizing Justin. He said that Justin yelled out, "Uncle Dave, I'm right here." David heard the loud silence on my end of the phone, so he changed the subject from Justin's appearance and let me know he fed them and bought them sweatshirts, because it was cold. He told me he loved me and assured me Justin would figure it out. I thanked him and hung up the phone, feeling empty inside.

Dillon has tried numerous times. He hasn't told me details, but I know he has been in touch with Justin and that he has done everything in his power to help his brother, but even Dillon can't save him at this point. My only hope is that seeing Dillon would remind Justin of who he used to be and that it might have some lasting impact. Martha's husband (Justin's Uncle Ed) has tried as well, but Justin always ends up right back on the streets doing the same thing. He gets himself out of one mess only to jump into more messes. No matter how many people try to help, and no matter how much love is poured out to him, Justin always goes back to chasing dope.

I'm fairly certain Justin's father has made a few attempts to help, and there may have been others, but it doesn't appear that any progress is being made. Justin is still out there, living on the streets deep in his addiction, and I know he's running out of time.

"THE HUMAN HEART IS THE MOST
DECEITFUL OF ALL THINGS, AND
DESPERATELY WICKED. WHO REALLY
KNOWS HOW BAD IT IS."

Jeremiah 17:9

Counting Spoons

MAKE ME GOOD AGAIN

CHAPTER
SIXTEEN

JUSTIN

This is a dark and wicked life I'm living, but I'm making my way. I have seven cities in my weekly rotation, and I hit one every day. I steal whatever I can get my hands-on, including bikes, shoes, clothing, and drug store stuff: beauty products, tools, video games, and controllers. I try not to go to any store more than once every few weeks because I don't want them to recognize me. I know I look like a homeless junkie, and sometimes I feel like I am exactly that, but there's something about when you do meth; it gives you an inflated sense of yourself, and you get really brave and confident—like you're invincible.

Between riding BART and walking, I cover a lot of territory. I catch the train going back and forth between Berkeley, Pleasanton, Union City, and Oakland. Before the sun goes down, I bring back my inventory, cash it out with my contact in Oakland, and then I'm set for dope, ice cream, and whatever else I need. It's that simple, but sometimes I get busted. A few times a month, I get arrested and spend the night in jail, and then I get released, so it's no big deal. I have probation violations everywhere, but the jails are overcrowded, and they don't hold drug offenders like me for very long.

At a store in Union City, I got my hands on a bunch of barber shop hair and beard trimmers that are popular and easy to sell on the street. I make some quick money selling them, and then Eric and I spend close to forty-eight hours high on meth. We are tweaking hard and come up with an idea. We get a pair of the trimmers and decide we are going to cut our hair and line ourselves up, nice and clean. We take turns sitting under a streetlight and spend hours getting our hair just right. I end up with a shaved head. A couple days later, I catch a glimpse of myself in a gas station mirror, and even though I am still high as a kite, I am shocked at my reflection. I don't even recognize myself. I look like an alien with gray skin and big, hollow eyes. Later that day I lift a beanie and start wearing it until my hair grows out again. When I first came out here, a lot of people said I looked like I didn't belong, but I don't get that anymore. Now I look like the hundreds of others out here on the streets, hustling and trying to survive.

There's a lot of people out here that have become like family to me. There's a group that usually camps out under the bridge and they're around my age. Most of them are addicts, some have mental health issues, and others are just down on their luck with no place to call home. I try to make my way there weekly and just hang out and help with whatever I can because I know they'd do the same for me. I can always stay there if I need to. I try to hit the parks weekly and pay my respects to the OG's that gather there. These guys have been out here on the streets and in the game for a long time, and you don't ever do them dirty; you treat them right, and they will have your back. Showing respect to the OG's comes in the form of cookies, coffee, candy, or their favorite malt liquor, and sometimes I just sit and talk to them. Everyone has a story to tell, and I like listening. I guess the street is just like any other community; after a while you recognize people, and you try to get a sense of them and see what they're about, and then sometimes you become friends. There's so much bad out here, that it's good to have people that you can talk to and care about.

Taking care of myself on the street is hard, but I have certain things that I always do. Every single day, I eat ice cream; it's like the only food I crave, and it's just so good. My favorite is the It's-It® Mint Chip ice cream sandwiches, but they're hard to steal, so I save my money for those and usually steal the six packs of Snickers® and Twix® ice cream bars because they're long and thin and easy to grab. At least two or three times a month, I go to this Day Center they have in downtown Oakland. You can take showers, do laundry, and they offer snacks, bottled water, and coffee. You can also get kits for shooting dope, which really surprised me. I guess they think it's better to give out free sterile kits than having people sharing needles and spreading disease.

I keep toothpaste, a toothbrush, deodorant, and other hygiene stuff in a Ziplock® bag in my pocket. When you're always on the move, you have to try and keep your necessities with you wherever you go. I also manage to get phones from the Obama Phone stands; they're free and you can make in-state calls, so that way I can call my mom and check in. I don't know why I do it because it always makes me feel bad, but I have to keep some sort of contact with my family, so I don't forget who I used to be. Sometimes I can't remember what life was like before drugs, and that scares me. I like to keep my family and memories close in my mind, so I don't ever lose them completely. I know it sounds weird, but those calls to my mom are important to me.

There's a lot to be scared of out here, and you have to be careful where you sleep. Eric and I go to hospital emergency waiting rooms or try to find places that are secluded. There was one night that Eric and I were fried; we'd been up for two or three days, and we needed to crash, badly. There is a park across town that has a cinder block fence around the dumpsters, and we found a place there that kept us out of sight from the street. We finished what was left of our dope. I was exhausted, and I passed out quickly. I'm not sure how long I was asleep, but I woke up to someone kicking me in the side. I jumped up and opened my eyes to the face of a little kid with a gun pointed at me. He couldn't have been older than twelve or thirteen. Eric started trying to talk to him, but I jumped the cinder block fence and got the hell out of there, running as fast as I could. I kept yelling at Eric to run, but I didn't hear him behind me. As I was running, I glanced back and saw that Eric was finally running too, but the kid was right behind him with the gun still pointed. I ran right; Eric ran left, and I saw a car full of guys pulling up, so he was blocked between the car and the kid, and I knew it was over for him. He was not going to live through this. There's so much weird stuff that happens here; I don't know what those guys wanted with us but knew something bad was about to go down. A lot of people out here are armed with guns, but we're not. I kept running, but hesitated in my steps because I didn't want to leave my buddy, but I didn't know how to help him. I just kept going and glancing back in his direction. I know the same kind of thing could happen to me at any time. If Eric dies, should I contact his family? I realize if either of us died, our families would never know what really happened to us. The thought makes me sick to my stomach. It seems like this kind of stuff happens all the time; every week there's some kind of near-death situation and it makes me wonder if we will make it out of here alive.

This is my life now, and it's intense. I find myself drawn to anything that brings adrenaline or gives me a rush. As much as I hate parts of how I'm living, I've also grown to actually like some of it. Each high and rush keeps me from facing reality, so I'm always searching for something. It doesn't matter if it's good or bad, just something to keep my mind occupied.

Man, oh man, our families must wonder what the hell is wrong with us. Both he and I come from good and loving homes, but we screwed up; drugs changed us.

When I'm high, I tend to think about my family, and I love talking about them to anyone on the street that will listen. I feel a lot of pride about where I came from. I talk a lot about my older brother Dillon; I've always admired his dedication to baseball, and now he's getting paid to play in a professional league. He's a strong athlete, and I know he's gonna do big things in life, and I love that. Talking about Dillon usually leads to me talking about my glory days in sports; I could have been just like my brother and gotten college scholarships, but I liked drugs too much. I talk about my mom, dad, my sister, my dog, and I even quote scripture, and share my love for Christ. I was saved in rehab at Teen Challenge, which is hard to admit, because of where I am now. When I'm high, I love to talk about all that stuff, but when I come down, when the high starts wearing off, I don't think about any of those things because it wrecks me. It turns me inside out, and I can't stand it, so I try to stay high all the time, and if I'm not high, then I'm figuring out how I'm gonna get my hands on more dope.

The sun is up, and I wake to it in full blown withdrawals. The day before, I came up on five bags of heroin. I hid behind a delivery truck in a parking lot to shoot it. I contemplated saving a few bags for the morning, but instead I put it all in one shot and blacked out. Now I'm lying behind a Mexican Restaurant, and it's morning. I know it's at least 10:00 a.m., because the restaurant is open. I must have blacked out for an entire day. One of the workers comes out the back door of the restaurant, sees me and starts yelling at me in Spanish, so I get up and start walking. I don't want any problems, so I take off running and end up at the park down the street.

I drop onto the grass in the shade under a tree. I'm sweating, and my stomach is cramping bad, my bones ache. I bury my face in my hands and can feel my pointed cheek bones. They feel like my hip bones look; like a sharp rock is protruding from underneath my skin. I get up and try to pee, but nothing comes out. Seems like I only piss once a day, and it smells strong, like it's concentrated. I don't think I've pooped in weeks. I guess I should try to eat something other than ice cream and drink some water occasionally. I feel empty. Everything hurts right now, including my heart. It's times like this that the reality of life hits me, and I fall apart. I start bawling. What happened to me? I think of my family and all that I've left behind, and I can't take it. I am terrified of this feeling. I'd rather face anything on the streets than this fear and emptiness. Everything inside of me aches; the physical and emotional pain is more than I can handle, and I feel like giving up, but I have to pull myself together. I have to!

I lean against the tree and take inventory. I have no money, dope, food, or drink, and I don't have a phone. On top of the aches in my bones, the bottom of my feet, and my thighs are killing me. I need to peel off my socks and sweats at some point, but not until I can get to a shower. I pull down the right side of my sweatpants just a little so I can inspect the sores; they're bright red and oozing with pus. They're stuck to my sweats, and it hurts so bad I want to scream. I think about how my legs got so messed up and it makes me want to crawl into a hole and die. Last week when Eric and I were tweaking, I told him I had a sore on my thigh from a needle; he looked at it and said it was an ingrown hair, so the meth told me to pluck and dig out as many hairs on my thighs as I could, and I went at it for hours. At the time, in my spun-out brain, it seemed like the right thing to do, but now I'm

163

covered in sores from digging into my own skin with tweezers. I don't know why I let everything get so out of control; I never thought it would get this bad, but it's *soooo* bad. I know I've done this to myself, and it sickens me.

I remember that Eric is probably dead, and I wish I could trade places with him. I don't know what to do, and I realize I'm running out of options. I wipe my face, pull myself to my feet, and try to suck it up. I need to get high and then everything will be okay again. I just need the brown warmth to heal me inside so I can feel alive. I start crying again, and I hate myself. I remember there is a God in the heavens who is supposed to love me no matter how far I fall, but I'm afraid maybe I've fallen too far for even Him. I feel so ashamed. There is nothing good left in me. I remember reading something that said that guilt tells us that we've done something wrong; shame tells us that *we are* wrong. What can I do when I know I'm bad? I feel like I'm going to just disappear at some point, and maybe that's what I want to happen. Maybe I'll just slowly waste away until there is nothing left of me.

I shake my head and squeeze my eyes shut trying to find some strength, and I do. I find enough to get up and start walking to my dealer, so he can front me enough to go hustle today. Knowing that relief is just four blocks away helps me keep moving, but I'm weak and fighting back tears as I walk, and, for the first time in a long time, I pray for God to make me good again; please, oh God, just make me good.

"BUT IF WE CONFESS OUR SINS TO HIM,
HE IS FAITHFUL AND JUST TO
FORGIVE US OUR SINS AND TO CLEANSE
US FROM ALL WICKEDNESS."

1 John 1:9

CHAPTER
SEVENTEEN

KATHRYN

My person and best friend since birth is my sister, Martha. She's two and a half years older than I am. We don't look alike, and we certainly don't act alike, but we have the same voice and mannerisms. Martha is a beautiful, free spirited, positive, funny, and charming person. She never gets mad; she just stays positive and spreads light and love wherever she goes. I'm not exaggerating when I say that *everyone* loves Martha; they just do.

It's April 2015, and Martha and I make a plan to go to church camp. It's actually a weekend Christian women's retreat, but I call it "church camp." Anyway, it sounds like a good idea, so we sign up at the gentle nudging of Cindy. Cindy is my boss but also happens to be a close friend and a devout Christian. Cindy knows I need something; she sees my pain and encourages me to go, so I sign us up and pay the deposit. The day comes, and I want to cancel. Justin is still on the streets and I am a complete wreck, but for some reason I don't cancel, and Martha and I pack our bags and head to the mountains.

The drive is horrendous. I am gripping the steering wheel like it is the only thing keeping me alive. We stop at a Denny's to eat, and all I can do is obsess about how dirty the place seems to me. Martha shrugs off my comments and says its fine, so we order. I continue inspecting the place and glance in the kitchen, silently wondering if the cook washed his hands. Martha is busy enjoying her food and looking at me like I am crazy, which is sort of true. I only mention Denny's to give you a glimpse of where my head is at; it isn't good. I am on the edge of something, and I feel like I am about to break.

We finally arrive at our destination in the beautiful redwoods of the Santa Cruz mountains. The air is crisp and smells of better, happier times. We grab our stuff, check into our room, and then go to the cafeteria for dinner. The neon-lighted cafeteria smells of food and hums with the chatter of what sounds like hundreds of voices. Voices of women who look happy and are all smiles, and it completely freaks me out. I want to turn around and leave right then, but Martha talks me into staying. I haven't slept well. I have no appetite, and I'm feeling suffocated. I avoid conversation, while Martha, true to her loving spirit, is braiding her hair, picking flowers, skipping along, and talking to every single person. Well, maybe she isn't skipping, but to me it feels like she is skipping. In some ways, it is perfect, because I feel like she balances the standoffish, anxiety-ridden vibe I am clearly giving off. I stay with Martha every second, not realizing that she only came for me.

We go to the classes, listen to the presenters, and it's good—comforting even. We visit and have our meals with our friends and sisters-in-faith, Cindy and Rosemary. I am quiet and don't say much, but it doesn't seem to matter to them. They are kind and supportive and don't push me. They just love me gently with no expectation of anything in return, and it is exactly what I need.

We go to a class called "Celebrate Recovery" (CR), and while making our way to the class, a young lady walks up and looks panicked. She asks us if we know where the CR class is, and we tell her that's where we're going too, so we walk together. The young lady looks as bad as I feel, and I find myself wondering what her story is. We walk in the classroom and take a seat in the chairs that are arranged in a circle. I immediately decide that I'm not participating in anything, and I didn't. A participatory exercise comes up; I pass and say I don't have my glasses and can't read, so they move on to Martha. She looks at me, mortified that I passed, and I feel like I am going to cry.

When the time came to share why we were there, the young

lady that we walked in with starts talking. As I listen, I feel like I am frozen in my chair, and I cannot stop staring at her. She describes the urge to use heroin; she cries and says she has two babies at home and every day she wants to get in her car and leave them and go find some dope. She cries because she doesn't think she is strong enough to resist and is scared about what she might do when she goes back home. The other women in the room are encouraging and supportive, and they praise her for coming and sharing. They lift her up and love her with no judgment or condemnation. I'm looking around the room, listening and taking it all in, and I'm shocked. How could she share that with all these strangers? What will happen to her and her babies? How completely awful! And when it is my turn, I pass once again. This young lady is courageous; she is terrified and reaching out for support. Good for her. She is the wise one. I just sit there in silence the entire time and try to focus on breathing and not breaking down; it is taking all I have left in me just to accomplish that.

The last evening during worship, I get goosebumps. The phone buzzing in my pocket goes unanswered. It buzzes again; I look at the call, see that it's Justin, and I don't answer it. I close my eyes, sway to the music, and lift my hands. I feel a tiny bit of peace. The Holy Spirit is lifting me up and letting me know I am still alive. I am alive, at "church camp," breathing, looking up, and feeling okay. The anxiety long forgotten, I sing with the worship music and feel a smile on my face. I'm not sure if I am actually smiling on the outside, but I am totally smiling on the inside.

FULL SURRENDER

EIGHTEEN

KATHRYN

Many people can tell you when they were saved and accepted Christ as their Savior, but I cannot. There have been many times in church when I raised my hands, professed my sins, and called Jesus into my heart, and waited. And when the next opportunity came, I would do it again, just to make sure Christ heard me. Then I would expectantly wait for some kind of verification that I was, in fact, saved. I would literally ask Christ to save me every chance I got, hoping that at least one of those times would stick. Sounds crazy, I know, but I knew I needed Jesus, and it seemed like a logical approach at the time. But let's talk about surrender. I absolutely can tell you when I surrendered my life, my will, my perceived control, my shame, my pain, my burdens, my Justin, my everything, to my Savior, Jesus Christ.

It is late at night. I'm in bed next to Darwin and we're both reading, trying to relax and settle into the night, when my phone rings. It's Santa Rita Jail with a collect call from Justin, asking will I accept the charges. Yep, I'll accept the charges. In all the dozens of times Justin was arrested prior to this time, he never called me to bail him out, not even once, which, in retrospect, is odd. I think he fit in when he was in jail, and it was just part of the life he had gotten used to.

Anyway, I accept the charges and listen to Justin asking me to bail him out. He got "rolled" the night before; he is in a cell with gang members and has been getting warnings all day that he is going to get hurt that night. Suddenly everything seems to slip into slow motion. I tell him, "No, I won't do it," but my voice is cracking and sounds weak; he says he has to call me back. We hang up, I look at Darwin and ask him what to do. He says, "Whatever you want, we will do it." I'm trembling and thinking there is no way I'm going to go get Justin, and, at the same time, wondering how quickly I can get to him.

I call Jason from my church, the one who told me about The Mission House. He is a godly man and has been a strong support for me; he answers my call and I quickly tell him what's going on. He surprises me with his answer. He tells me to bail Justin out or tell him to ask to be put in protective custody. He continues on about how it isn't right, and Justin needs to be safe, and I stop hearing his words. I stop listening because I already know I will not pick him up. I am certain of that. We hang up and within ten minutes, the phone rings again, and I accept the charges. I feel my pulse in my temples, and the sobs are starting, but they are buried. Buried deep, below the surface of my skin, so you can't hear them. But I feel them rising in me. I tell Justin to go to protective custody, and I already know what his response will be. He can't. "That's something you just don't do, Mom." I realize my son is street; he has a community of criminals that he is part of, and they don't go into protective custody. The reality of his mindset rattles me. I respond with, "You're in just as much danger in jail as you are on the streets, so I'm not sure what to tell you." He doesn't plead or ask again, he just says, "Okay, I understand, I love you, Mom," and then hangs up. The dial tone is there, but I'm still holding the phone—unable to release it. My heart is pounding in my chest, and my thoughts are racing; is that it? Is that the last time I will talk to my son? Will he die tonight? I'm scared, but I don't regret my decision; I know it was the right thing to do.

I don't think I'm breathing, so I tell myself to breathe, and then it happens. I start to unravel. I break. I close the door to the spare room I'm in, lying on my side and sobbing, but not allowing any sound to come out. I don't want Darwin to hear this. I don't want to feel this. I realize that I can't do it anymore; I'm depleted. I have nothing left to hold on to; I am completely wrecked, so I look up and plead to a God I don't know. I surrender it all to Him. I cry out for God to help me, help Justin, God please, please, PLEASE help us!

I don't know how long I am in that room. Could have been thirty minutes or four hours, I don't know, but at some point, I gather myself up, wash my face, dab my swollen eyes with a cold rag, and slip back into bed without making a sound. I hear the steady breath of my boyfriend as he is sleeping, and I'm so grateful to lie next to this strong and loving man. The thought of him and how he has stood by me makes me teary all over again, but I stop myself from crying and just lie on my side, close my eyes, and pray.

I barely sleep at all that night and remember seeing the sunrise, and I am surprised by it. Turns out, the sky didn't fall in. I haven't gotten a phone call that my son is dead. Everything seems the same. I'm not sure when exactly it happens but slowly, very slowly in the days and weeks to come, I start to feel different. Justin survives the nights in jail and goes right back to the streets, still deep in his addiction and life of crime, but as for me? Well, I sort of start living again. I don't pass on all the food—I eat more and enjoy it. I start putting creamer in my coffee to taste its goodness, and I stop jumping out of my skin when the phone rings. I don't sleep much but I do sleep, and the nightmares stop. And when Justin calls, it doesn't destroy me. I mean, don't get me wrong; I am still hurting. I am hurting badly. But I don't feel like I am going to die. God is giving me a taste of peace; He is calming my heart and letting me rest in His grace.

But Justin doesn't get better. In fact, things get worse. I think the Lord is testing my faith, and, while I am not even close to being okay, I am not dying. I know I'm going to survive.

SIX TACOS, ONE MILKSHAKE, AND A PLANE

CHAPTER
NINETEEN

KATHRYN

It's a Wednesday afternoon as I sit in my office staring at my computer screen, and I feel like I'm in a trance. I try to shake it off and look away from my computer, only to catch myself staring out of my office window into the sky. It feels like the world is quiet and I am all alone, lost in my thoughts. Work is the same, the normal hustle of the day is happening with the typical noises in the hallway of people walking by; the copy machine down the hall is humming, people are talking, doors are opening and closing, phones are ringing—and I'm oblivious to it all. It's like background noise that is drowned out by the loud thoughts in my head. Questions keep rolling around in my mind; *What is Justin doing? What will happen to him? What will happen to me? How long has it been since he's been out on the street? How much longer can he last? Why am I still sitting here?*

I snap out of the trance and know I've got to do something. I don't bother cleaning off my desk, I just grab my stuff and rush out of my office and don't stop walking as I ask a team member to cancel my afternoon meetings. As I'm rushing to my boss's office, I ask a team member to shut down my computer and lock my office door, "Please Dawn, I don't have time. I have to go now." I get to my boss's door, knock, and quickly open it. Cindy is sitting with a co-worker and friend I call Schumacher. I interrupt them, "I have to go."

Cindy responds, "Okay, is everything alright?"

I tell her, "No, um yes, actually I don't know, but I have to do something. I'm going to find Justin."

She looks surprised and calmly asks "Okay, do you need help? I mean, what are you going to do?"

I'm already walking away, feeling a rush of adrenaline and my heart beating fast in my chest.

"I'm not sure, but I have to go. I have to hurry, but yeah, I'm good! I'll see you tomorrow."

Schumacher follows me as we pass her office and stop. She looks at me and asks with great concern, "What do you need?" I tell her nothing, but she sees me shaking and says, "Just be careful, okay? We're here if you need us." I'm blinking hard, so I don't cry, because this is not the time to break down.

I walk as fast as I can, almost jogging, down the hall and outside to my car. I throw my briefcase and purse in the back seat, jump in the car, buckle my seat belt, and start the engine. With both hands on the steering wheel, eyes closed, taking slow, deep breaths, I pray for God to give me strength. Somehow I will find Justin. I don't know how, I just know I need to go now.

I get on the freeway and start heading to the Bay Area. I'm watching my speed limit because the last thing I need is a ticket, but I have got to get there fast. I turn on worship music, with the volume up as loud as it will go, hoping the words will fill me with hope and conviction. I don't really have a plan and have no idea what I'm doing, but I'm going anyway. I am certain that something is going to happen today. I don't know if it's good or bad, but this madness has got to end. Something must change! "God please help me; please help me find my son." I barely remember the forty-five-minute drive through Modesto, Manteca, and Tracy. I see the windmills as I'm driving over the Altamont Pass on my way to Livermore, then through Dublin, and past Castro Valley. I merge onto 880, headed to Oakland, and my phone rings. It's a number I don't recognize but I quickly answer it anyway. I can barely hear Justin's voice.

"Mom? Mom! Please, it's me, please, I need help, I can't do it anymore, I'm done, I just need. . ."

Strength has replaced the fear I was holding inside my chest, and my voice is strong and steady when I respond, "Justin, I'm on my way, Son. I'm in the Bay Area right now, I'm here for you. I'm coming, stay right where you are honey, everything is going to be alright,..." and I know it is. Nothing is going to stop me from getting to my son today. I keep praying to my Savior who I know is listening.

"God please keep Justin safe, free him from bondage, God please deliver Justin." I forget the speed limit and drive as fast as I can to get to my son, the entire time repeating out loud in a voice just above a whisper, "God please keep him safe, free and deliver him; keep him safe, free and deliver him; please just keep him safe, free and deliver him..."

JUSTIN

It's August 2015. I'm sitting, more like slumping, on the cement walkway in front of Safeway in San Leandro, California. I'm depleted, worn, and barely hanging on. I've got sores on my feet from walking in shoes that are falling apart. I haven't showered, eaten, slept, or had any dope for a while. By "a while" I mean it could have been an hour or maybe a few days; I have no sense of time. Eric turned up a few weeks ago, he wasn't dead after all, but we got separated again, and I have no idea where he is. I am alone—completely alone.

As I sit here watching people walk around me, each of them being careful not to make eye contact with the homeless, deranged scumbag I know I appear to be, I hurt so deeply. Not just my body, but my heart and soul hurt. I long to be loved, to be cared for, and to be somebody again. I weep until I have no more tears. I ache for a hand, a touch, or a kind voice to acknowledge my existence. I'm looking and praying for a miracle. Whether that miracle is dope, food, or salvation, I'm not sure I even care. I just know I cannot take it anymore.

I lie on the ground, pleading with God to give me a life worth living, because I am tired of this; I have no strength left. I have come to the point of death, or a life that God is going to lead, those are my two options. I take my phone out of my pocket and see that it is still charged. I call my mom. And ... she answered her phone! I don't know what I said, but it was something like, "Mom, please come get me, I'm done, I'm ready, please, please, please..." I don't think she even heard the second "please" before she told me she was in her car looking for me at that very moment. She was in the Bay Area looking for me. God is good, God is sovereign, and He will never forsake you.

Mom and I make a plan to meet at the BART Station in San Leandro, next to the Bay Fair Mall. My heart is racing, and all I can think about is crawling into the safety of her car. Maybe I will hustle money from her, get some food, or talk her into getting me a hotel room and build up my strength for a bit. Maybe I would go to rehab again. Maybe she won't show. At this point I have no idea what I am going to do past getting into her car. I gather what's left of my strength and start walking toward the station. I'm trying hard to stay calm; I can't think of anything other than getting in her car.

I make it to the BART parking lot and stop dead in my tracks when I see my mom. She's standing next to a cop, and his lights are flashing. She called the cops? This is a set up? What? I don't understand. Why would she do this? I wait and wait, until finally the cop leaves, and then I call her. I watch her answer the phone; her voice is shaky.

"Justin! Where are you? I can't believe what just happened. A drunk driver drove into my car and took off, but not before I got a picture of him and his license plate. Man, oh man, he picked the wrong day to get in my way. I kind of lost it. When he was driving away, I threw my shoe at his car...um, I mean this guy looked rough! I probably should not have done that. Never mind that, tell me where you are, Son."

Just to be certain she didn't call the cops, I lie to her again and say I got tied up and to meet me at Rite Aid. I make it to the store and stay back a bit until I see her drive up, and then I wait. All is quiet. Mom is alone, and no cops are in sight, so I head in her direction.

She doesn't look at me with disgust like she usually does, it's like she's on a mission, and there is no time to spare. She tells me to get in the car and without hesitation, I do. As I settle my filthy, depleted body into the seat, something in me shifts. I roll my window down and feel the warmth of the sun on my face. The wind gently washes over my skin as I rest my head back in my seat. I feel safe for the first time in months, and I'm ready for a change.

I'm not going to lie or hustle today. I'm not going to look for dope. I'm going to sit in this car with my mom and go, willingly, wherever it is she thinks we need to go. I can't pray yet, but I'm looking up and not down. Is there hope? Can I really be okay again? I'm going to try. I am really going to try.

Kaiser Emergency Room is the plan, so Mom drags me inside. As I am being triaged, Mom pulls no punches running down our situation. She tells the nurse in a voice I don't think I've heard before, "He's an addict, and he's been homeless for months. He's dehydrated and sick and we need help . . . Please!" They rush me in and start an IV to get some fluids in me. I will never forget that moment of lying in the hospital bed with two nurses trying to find a good vein. I lay there looking down at my body in the hospital gown as the cold hands of the nurses squeezed my arms and my legs trying to find a vein. I see the sores on my legs a half-inch deep, the track marks going up my inner thighs and down my arms, and my skinny, broken body, and it hits me hard. I cannot live this way anymore; I've got to get clean and stay clean. I have to! In the bright lights of the emergency room, everything feels and looks different than it does when you're out on the street. I realize that I've destroyed my own body, and it's an ugly reality. How could I do this to myself?

They eventually find a vein in my chest and start the IV. In my head I can't help but chuckle at the fact that there is a needle pumping something healthy into my veins for once. As the fluids start to enter my body, it feels good. The nurse helping us is amazing. I don't feel like she is judging me, in fact she is encouraging. I am so used to being looked down upon, that when the nurse fixes her eyes on mine, I feel love and warmth so pure that I want to cry. I'm not sure how the subject came up, but the nurse and my mom get to talking, confirm that we are all believers, and the nurse asks if she can pray for me. I say "Yes, please." We all hold hands and bow our heads, and she leads us in prayer. As my mom and the nurse talk next steps, I am struck by the fact that I am not thinking about drugs. I am calming down and still determined to get help. Knowing this is a critical time, that "window" when an addict is ready, you must move fast, so mom is moving fast, and so is the nurse, and so is my Savior. God is opening doors, and I am walking through them.

Next step is Kaiser detox. This will be my fifth time. There are no beds, so mom asks to speak to whoever is in charge. The lady in charge is professional and straightforward, and she is also kind. She says to give her twenty-four hours and they will find me a bed.

Mom and I get food and drinks and stay in a hotel until the next morning. I'm trying to sleep and feel my bones aching. I want to say I stayed strong, but I didn't. I remember a tiny bag of dope hidden in my sock, so I sneak into the bathroom and shoot enough heroin to get me through the night. I don't think either of us slept much, but the next morning we head back to the lady in charge, and she tells us we're good to go; there's a bed.

Back in detox, I am greeted by the staff as if I'm a regular, which is not a good feeling. Being a regular is cool when it's at a local pub or gym, but at a detox facility? Not so much. I get searched and put my belongings in the locker. Gotta make sure there are no shoelaces or hoodies with strings, because sometimes desperate people try to hang themselves in detox. Within a few hours, I get to see my counselor, Chuck, who immediately remembers me. Even though this is a secular detox facility, Chuck is a devout Christian. He prays with me and lets me know he and his wife have been praying for me since the last time I was sitting in his office. I'm not sure why he would do that for me, but I'm so grateful.

When detoxing, the first three days are the worst. If you can get through those three days, you have a chance at getting clean. I keep waiting to feel like death, but I don't. I am not ready to run a marathon or anything, but I am also not feeling very dope sick. By day five you can make phone calls and have visitors, so when Mom asks me if I need anything, I ask her to bring lots of candy.

Before visiting hours, I sit at the edge of my cot with my head in my hands. I still haven't really prayed or acknowledged the Lord. I just can't seem to find the words. I am also worrying about the test I have to take. I am trying to get into Teen Challenge (for the third time), and in order to do that I need to have blood work done to make sure I don't have HIV or Hepatitis or any other communicable disease that addicts on the street often contract. They took blood that morning, and results would be in by day's end. The very thought of the results makes me nervous, so I decide to make a deal with the Lord. If my test results come back clean, which isn't likely, I will get on my knees and honestly repent, and I'll probably do the same thing if the test results are dirty, but I'm hoping for a miracle. The day seems to drag, and, after a few hours, my mom shows up. She's got candy in hand and as she's walking in, my counselor pokes his head out of his office, meets my eyes and says, "Hey J, you're clean."

I freeze. "Wait, what?"

He repeats, "You're clean buddy, the blood work is clear." His ear-to-ear grin tells me that he is for real; he isn't kidding. I look at him, he looks at me, and then he looks up, back at me and gives a quick nod. I know what he means; he's telling me to keep my eyes fixed on God because He is starting to work in me.

Mom isn't entirely sure what is happening until I explain the blood tests and my promise to God about prayer. My hands are shaking, and I have tears streaming down my face at the reality of my test results, no diseases. Wow. Just wow.

I'm eating a snickers, probably my fourth candy bar. Side note: when addicts are detoxing, they want candy, chocolate, soda, and coffee in large amounts. Anyway, a lady about my mom's age (she is detoxing too) walks in and tells my mom what a great job she has done raising me and what a joy I am to have around. Mom looks even more confused, and I can almost hear her thoughts; *My son is in detox, coming off heroin and meth, and I'm getting compliments on my parenting.... what in the world is going on?* Mom is also confused about how I look. I am eating, sleeping, and feel okay; my color is good, and my eyes are clear. Why am I not feeling dope sick? She is confused, but I'm not. For the first time in a while, I feel a stirring of the Holy Spirit in me.

I take my time eating dinner, dreading getting on my knees and asking for forgiveness. I mean, where do I even start? How do I ask forgiveness for all that I've done? It's overwhelming, and I wonder how God can forgive someone like me. I take my time eating dinner, wander the halls for a bit, chat with some of the new friends I've made here, call Dillon, and finally make my way back to my room. Then I close my eyes, take a long, deep breath, bow down and begin to pray. I pray until my knees ache. I pray and repent for my sins and ask God for forgiveness over and over, and then I thank God and praise Him until all my tears are shed. I rise to my feet, eat another candy bar, brush my teeth, and sleep soundly for the first time in forever.

As the sun comes up, I can smell coffee brewing. I throw on my sweatshirt, run my fingers through my hair, and go to the cafeteria. My first cup of coffee is strong and black and thick enough to choke on, and it is amazing. As I am eating my breakfast of oatmeal and soggy toast, I realize I am smiling. This is a good day. This is another day off the streets, and I am a blessed man.

My seven day detox ends, and Mom lets me know that Teen Challenge in Sacramento has a bed. Instructions are to pick me up and go straight to Teen Challenge. No stops ANYWHERE. My mom has taken me to rehab many times, and every time I was high as a kite. I would make an excuse that I needed to use the restroom and come out twenty minutes later nodding out and feeling good from the heroin I had hidden in my sock. It was always my "last hurrah" before rehab or detox. This never went well and was probably some of the worst experiences that Mom had to deal with in my addiction. Because of this I don't ask her to stop anywhere; I know better. We do go to the store right before we get to Teen Challenge to get the basics: toothbrush and paste, t-shirts, deodorant, the works. Mom always buys way more than what is necessary, but I don't say anything because I appreciate it so much. I have gone without for so long that it feels good to be cared for.

We arrive at Teen Challenge, park the car, and sit in silence for just a few minutes. I look up at the familiar house and reflect on the first time I came here just two years ago. Scared, young, and naïve to the streets. It was what I needed then, but is it what I need now? I quickly decide it doesn't matter. I am in. I am ready. Mom and I hug; she cries, I do my best to smile, and we part ways. She drives home probably exhausted, and relieved I'm in a secure environment.

I'm hungry and a bit nervous, but still ready. I'm still motivated, still trusting that God has a plan for me. The drill is the same, just new faces this time. Search your stuff, show you around, assign a bunk. Eat, pray, eat, sleep, and try to gain some strength. My stomach rumbles, and I puke a bit, feeling the sickness of detox a little more. I read the Bible and get into God's Word, and I start to feel lighter. Hopeful. Even peaceful.

Then I get the call. Mom tells me there is a bed open at The Mission

House in Washington, and I must decide what I want to do. The Mission House is a place that Jason, my mom's friend from church, told her about. Jason and I had talked a few times when I was on the streets. He was a graduate of The Mission House, and it sounds like a promising program. If I'm going to go, I have to get on a plane and get there within forty-eight hours or I will lose the spot. Mom tells me it is my decision, so "I need to pray about it, and I had better be right, because this is it!" This time had to stick! I hang up the phone and sit there thinking. I am doing well here; they are making a leader out of me already. I'm setting the example for others in the house with a promise at a potential job. I'm in downtown Sacramento, which is about one and a half hours from my family. It feels comfortable and good, and I'm not sure I want to give that up. I think about it and get on my knees and pray for the Lord to guide my steps.

I wake up the next morning and know I have to go. I call Mom and tell her I want to go to The Mission House, and she books the flight. I know this could be a mistake, but no matter what lies ahead in Washington, I will stick it out. And here's the thing, even in rehab I have to be successful. No matter what happens, I will not quit. God put it on my heart to go, and I must be obedient.

I pack my stuff, say my goodbyes, the guys pray over me, and I wait on the porch. My mom and her boyfriend drive up, and we load my things and head out. We stop to get some food from Jim Boy's Tacos in a strip mall in Sacramento. I'm starving and somehow devour six big tacos, and a strawberry milkshake with lots of whipped cream. We finish lunch and jump back in the truck and start the drive to the airport. My stomach is full, and my anxiety is starting to really kick in. I'm scared of what lies ahead. I have no idea what I am doing, but I know I have to succeed. But first let me back up to the night before. When I told mom I decided to go to Washington, she realized I had to fly, and I had no identification. She called the airlines, and they told her I wouldn't be able to fly. She called Jason, who told her to do her best to find something to use as identification and to pray, and then he told her to get some sleep and let God take it from there. Mom showed up today with two yearbooks, a birth certificate, my high school campus ID card, a library card, and a faded copy of an expired temporary ID. I would have laughed, but she looks so distressed, I just act like it is normal to take high school yearbooks to the airport to use as identification. At this point serious stress is happening. My heart is pounding; I see mom's hands trembling and Darwin is cracking jokes, which actually helps.

We get to the airport and get in line. Mom has all the crap in tow, and I have the expired, sorry-looking copy of an ID. The gentleman looks at my ticket and expired, faded ID, and tells me to enjoy my flight. I can hear my mom catch her breath, but I'm not surprised. God is at work; He is opening doors and I am following His lead. I board the plane.

"O LORD, I HAVE COME TO YOU FOR PROTECTION;

DON'T LET ME BE DISGRACED.

SAVE ME, FOR YOU DO WHAT IS RIGHT.

TURN YOUR EAR TO LISTEN TO ME;

RESCUE ME QUICKLY.

BE MY ROCK OF PROTECTION,

A FORTRESS WHERE I WILL BE SAFE.

YOU ARE MY ROCK AND MY FORTRESS.

FOR THE HONOR OF YOUR NAME,

LEAD ME OUT OF THIS DANGER.

PULL ME FROM THE TRAP

MY ENEMIES SET FOR ME,

FOR I FIND PROTECTION IN YOU ALONE.

I ENTRUST MY SPIRIT INTO YOUR HAND.

RESCUE ME, LORD,

FOR YOU ARE A FAITHFUL GOD."

Psalm 31:1-5

I AM RIGHT WHERE GOD WANTS ME

TWENTY

KATHRYN

I am in shock. I cannot believe they let him pass through security without a driver's license. I was prepared to go to battle with this airline, and I was equipped with documents to prove Justin's identity. I barely slept the night before in anticipation of this very moment when I was going to have to convince them that Justin's life depended on him getting on that plane. I realize that the time I spent on my knees in prayer was much more productive than the time I spent rummaging through paperwork, looking for something to show Justin's identity.

We walk up to security towards the gate to board the plane, and the gentlemen tells Justin to "Have a good flight." That's it. No questions, no hesitation, he just walks through. My heart is pounding so hard in anticipation of him getting rejected that when he goes through, all I can do is gasp, trying to get some air back in my lungs. It feels as if this journey in Justin's addiction has led us to this very moment and if he gets on that plane and goes to this program in Washington, he may have a chance at a life worth living. I have prayed for things to go smoothly and pleaded with God to get Justin on that plane. I'm not sure I believed it could happen, but Justin is indeed going to board that plane.

I am not prepared for the quick goodbye, so when Justin walks through security, I drop all my paperwork on the ground and go to him. We hug tightly for just a few seconds before he walks away. I watch him head towards the gate to board the plane until I can't see him anymore. With Darwin's help, I start gathering up his yearbooks and paperwork off the ground. I finally have everything picked up, and the tears start falling. A crew member from the airlines looks at me tenderly, smiles, and says, "Let me guess, are you sending your boy off to college? I know that can be tough."

This catches me by surprise. I stop in my tracks, laughing out loud. "Yeah, sure, something like that." Darwin and I smile at each other and start to leave, but my legs won't seem to move. He senses my hesitation and asks if I'd like to watch the plane leave, and I nod. In my head, I am once again thanking God for this man that always knows exactly what I need. We walk over to the window and plop down on the floor.

I look out to the runway, desperately trying to spot which plane he's on when Darwin, as if reading my thoughts, points it out to me. As I stare at the plane, everything else seems to disappear. Without allowing my eyes to look away, I quietly ask Darwin if he thinks Justin is on the plane or if he escaped and made a run for it. This makes us both laugh, and he assures me that my son is on the plane. I pretend that I'm kidding, but I wonder if Justin is really seated on that plane. I am happy, sad, tired, excited, and completely out of sorts.

As the plane slowly moves down the runway, we sit there and watch it gain speed. The lump in my throat gets bigger as the plane gets smaller and smaller, until it finally disappears behind the clouds. Darwin asks if I'm ready, and I say not quite. I don't know what I'm waiting for, but I need a few more minutes. People are walking by, and we just keep sitting there. I'm staring at the tiny spec in the sky and then watch it disappear. Part of me expects to see the plane turn around, come back, and drop Justin off, with a crew member saying there's been a mistake and they can't take him. I wonder why I want him on this plane so badly. Was it to get him out of state, or do I really believe the end of his suffering and the beginning of freedom is waiting for him in Washington? I'm not sure, but I feel like we've been preparing for this day for a long time, and now that it has happened and he's on his way, I'm having a hard time understanding why I don't feel any relief. I realize there is a lot that still needs to happen. The plane needs to get there, they need to find him and get him to the program, and then Justin needs to commit to doing the work. He has got to make it happen this time!

I don't allow myself to relax just yet. I text the Program Manager in Washington and tell him that Justin is on the plane. I also give him a description of my son and send him a picture of what he's wearing. While Justin was busy stuffing his face with those tacos, I took a few pictures of him so I could send them. I realize this was a bit irrational; I was acting like I was sending Justin out on his first field trip in grade school instead of helping my adult son get into a treatment facility, but it seemed like a logical thing to do at the time.

I finally feel okay to leave. I'm convinced the plane isn't going to turn around, and I'm ready to get home. We walk to the truck, and I text Jason who has been such a strong support for us during this journey. Instead of texting back, Jason immediately calls me, and I am surprised at the excitement in his voice. He is thrilled to hear that Justin is on his way to Washington. It has been a long road getting to this day. Jason is praising the Lord and asks me to keep him posted and says he will continue to pray for us. This is a huge step for Justin, and I'm starting to let the reality of it sink in.

We start driving, and as we get closer to home, I get a text message saying that they have Justin in the car, and they're on their way to The Mission House. Relief floods me. Okay, another step in the right direction. I exhale slowly, close my eyes, and lean back in my seat. The weight on my chest is starting to lighten. Darwin grabs my hand, gives it a quick squeeze, and we keep driving.

I haven't eaten all day and Darwin is insisting that I do, so we stop and get some food, and then my phone rings. I answer, and it's Justin. My heart starts pounding again in anticipation of what he has to say. Why is he calling me? Typically, programs don't allow it. I'm already prepared to tell him if he's not staying then he can figure out what to do next because I refuse to bring him back here. I manage to hold those thoughts in and instead say, "Hi Son, talk to me."

"Mom, I'm here, I'm exactly where I'm supposed to me. I have peace. Mom, please. You've got to listen! You've done everything you can; now it's up to me. Don't worry; I'm going to be fine. I am right where God wants me. The house is nice; they didn't search me or anything. They showed me to my room and gave me some time to get settled and call you. Thank you, thank you, thank you for everything. I love you so much. Please don't worry! I'm going to be fine. I love you, and I'll call you when I can."

We hang up. Darwin sees my reaction and asks if everything is alright.

"Yes, everything is good, he's right where he is supposed to be."

I take a deep, cleansing breath and feel a lightness in my body. I replay his words. . . "I am right where God wants me . . . you've done everything you can; now it's up to me . . . I love you so much." Over and over, I think about his words and the sound of his voice. He almost sounded frantic but in a good way; like he had an important message and had only a few minutes to get it all out. I feel like he needed me to hear every word and he desperately needed me to believe him. I think Justin knew that God was leading us, and he wanted me to be okay. He sounded grateful. He sounded confident and strong.

We pull up to our house and walk in. I throw all the paperwork on the couch, kick off my shoes, get a bottled water from the fridge, and tell Darwin I'll be upstairs. He asks if I need anything; I tell him I need a few minutes to myself. He understands this about me and generously gives me the time and space I need.

I walk upstairs to our bedroom and close the door behind me and lean against it. I close my eyes, exhale slowly, and look around our room. I step over to our neatly made bed, with the pillows all lined up perfectly and the warm throw blanket that is folded on the corner. I love our bed. I start my day by making it, and I don't return to it until my day is done, when I can crawl into the safety and warmth of it for the night.

I sit on the bed and lean against the pillows. I need to call my sister; I need to get ready for the week, and I need to let go and trust in the Lord. His hands have guided us to this place. Whether Justin makes it through this or not isn't up to me. There is nothing more I can do but pray. I need to let go and keep moving forward.

I make a list of things I need to get done and put the pen and paper down, and I just sit there on the edge of my bed looking out the window at the same blue sky I watched Justin's plane disappear into. I sit in the quiet and feel the goodness of it all, letting the peace fill me.

I won't hear from Justin during the blackout period, which is forty-five days, and I know that is a good thing. The distance between us is needed.

I replay Justin's words, "I am right where God wants me. . . . Thank you for everything. I love you so much. Please don't worry. . . . I'm going to be fine. I love you".

I say out loud to my youngest son with the big brown eyes, who is miles and miles away, "I'm right where God wants me too, Son. I love you so much."

Counting Spoons

YELLOW ROSES

CHAPTER

TWENTY ONE

KATHRYN

I love Darwin more than life itself, but our upcoming wedding with a guest list of two hundred people terrifies me.

Justin is settling in at The Mission House. He's in his blackout period, meaning he can't talk to anyone outside of the program and cannot attend our wedding. I'm at peace with that because I know he's exactly where he needs to be; I'm just having a hard time getting my head around the fact that our wedding day is just a few weeks away. I just don't feel like I've been able to catch my breath yet.

When we got engaged, Justin was doing well, and then the ground fell out from under us. We've lived in an ugly kind of chaos for most of this past year, but that is behind us now; it's time to move on.

The venue is booked. RSVPs have been received; flowers and food are ordered, and most everything is done, but it feels like we have thrown this thing together in a hasty kind of way. With all the drama surrounding Justin, I haven't been able to put my heart into planning this day for us, and I feel like Darwin has done most of the work. It just doesn't seem right.

Our wedding is scheduled for October 3, 2015, at four o'clock. Darwin knew I was stressed, so when he kisses me goodbye the day before our wedding, he tells me just to show up and be ready, and to leave the rest to him. He is so good to me. Many people didn't understand why we waited so long to get married, but to me, other than Justin not being able to come, the timing of our marriage feels perfect.

Dillon and Shay come early the morning of our wedding and make me breakfast. Shay sees my hands trembling and tells Dillon to make me a mimosa to calm my nerves, which he does, and it helps. I have my hair and make-up done and am as ready as I can get.

Since my father had passed, it seems fitting that Dillon will walk me down the aisle. He's always been a source of strength for me, and I am comforted knowing he will be there. Originally both Dillon and Justin were going to walk me down the aisle, but a lot has happened since our engagement a year ago.

Darwin's daughter Kayleigh, Shay, and Martha will be standing on my side. Dillon and Darwin's son, Justin Anthony, will stand on Darwin's side. Now, there will be one less person on Darwin's side; a big empty space where my youngest son was going to be standing. The thought makes me sad, and I wonder what all the guests will think when they don't see Justin at our wedding. I toss the thought away because I really don't care what anyone thinks. My son's battle with addiction is no one's business.

Martha asks what we will tell people, and I answer her firmly.

"Nothing, we don't have to tell anyone anything." Her expression tells me she doesn't approve but I don't really care; I am not talking to anyone about it.

We drive to the wedding site, and it's early. Darwin has a trailer delivered so I would have a place to get dressed and hang out until the ceremony starts, and I am thankful for that. I get out of the car and am surprised at what a beautiful day it is. I've been so nervous and lost in my thoughts that I hadn't noticed the sky of blue full of white puffy clouds and brilliant sunshine.

I go in the trailer and get my clothes out. My shoes are gorgeous—a lovely shade of silver with a high heel and ankle strap. My dress is hanging up by the window, and I realize I hadn't looked at it since I bought it. It's so pretty! Martha and I found it at the mall after about thirty minutes of shopping, and it was on sale for sixty dollars. When I tried it on and came out, the sales lady screamed and yelled at me,

"Ohhhhhh honey you have got to get that dress!" Martha had the same reaction, and I felt like it was made just for me. It's off-white and comes down to just above my knees, it's form fitting with a V-neck in the front and back. Even though I'm a bit thin, it fits me perfectly.

There's a knock on the door. I open it and see the sweet young lady that is doing our flowers. My request was for yellow roses. Everyone who knew me well would know that the yellow roses represent my mom, and I needed her memory to be with me today. Dad used to call her his "yellow rose of Texas," and it was the sweetest thing. I take one look at the beautiful bouquet of yellow roses that were just starting to open, and almost burst into tears at the beauty of them. They are just so lovely.

I suddenly become aware of how I've been acting, as if this ceremony is an obligation of some sort. I've been so caught up with everything that has happened with Justin, that I'm afraid I've missed the actual beauty and meaning of one of the most important days of my life. I am so humbled. I know that this big wedding in this beautiful setting was done for me. Darwin wanted me to experience the purity of our love and the celebration of our life together. I'm suddenly overwhelmed and so incredibly thankful for the blessing of this day.

I look in the mirror. My normally messy hair is blown dry, with waves lying across my shoulders, and it feels soft. My makeup is just right, and I feel pretty. Oh, my goodness, the reality of this day is starting to sink in. I'm going to marry Darwin!

There's a knock on the door, and my girls come and join me. I take the opportunity to tell them each how I feel about them and our incredible family. The words are coming quickly, and I'm full of emotion. We're all crying and trying hard not to ruin our make-up. I love these women so much, and I desperately want them to know it. I hear cars and voices, so Shay and I peek out of the window in the trailer. We shriek and giggle as guests start walking in. Oh wow, there are lots of people here! Of the 200 invitations we sent, we had 180 confirm. I smile, realizing how much I love all these people.

The barn is gorgeous. The ceilings are so high that they needed tall ladders to hang the white lights that were draped everywhere. There are three huge wooden chandeliers that hang high and burn with a brilliant glow. Each table has flowers and greenery displayed on cream-colored linens, with framed pictures of the Eiffel Tower and pictures of Paris, France. I wanted to add to the beauty of the barn, not take away from it so we kept it simple with just flowers, greenery, and everything else is neutral. As the sun goes down, the barn will have a warm glow surrounding it from all the lights that are streaming across the big wooden beams. The combination of the rustic beauty of the barn and the flowers is exquisite.

We all hug, and the girls leave me to take their places for the ceremony. I'm dressed and ready. There's a knock on the door—it's Dillon. I see him and panic a bit, and tell him I don't think I can do this in front of all these people. He tells me I absolutely can, and that he'll be right there with me.

He looks so handsome in his suit and my heart is grateful that he is here. I suddenly feel the loss of my brother Randy, who left us way too soon, and my mom and dad, and the weight of Justin's absence. I shake it off, find my strength, take a deep breath, and take Dillon's hand as he helps me walk down the stairs.

Dillon looks at me "You good, Mom?" I tell him yes, I'm good. He smiles his big, beautiful smile and says, "Then let's go get you married!" As we're walking toward the opening of the barn, I feel him look at me as he slows his step. "What is it, Son?" I hear him exhale slowly, he leans in towards me and quietly says "Man, Mom, it's just, you look amazing. You look so beautiful." I'm fighting back the tears, so I don't smear my make-up, but his words fill me with joy and for the first time, in a long time, I do feel beautiful.

We round the corner and stop for just a moment, and I hear the music start to play and the sound of 180 people rising to their feet to face us. I look around at all the people that showed up for us today, and I can barely take it in. I look down the aisle and see Darwin looking at me. He is so handsome and looks like he might cry, and I love him for it.

Dillon and I walk arm in arm slowly up the aisle. I look at all the smiling faces and I'm smiling back. There is only light and love in this place, and this moment is all that matters.

One of our best friends is officiating the wedding, and I feel like I'm beaming as I listen to him describe our love. I ask him to read 1 Corinthians 13:4–5 and as he recites the words, I know that this is the love I will forever share with this man that's about to become my husband. I am so happy.

It's time for our vows and Darwin goes first. He tells me I'm the love of his life and he can't wait to spend forever with me, and it's quickly over. Now it's my turn. I'm feeling a new sense of confidence, so I pull out my vows that I had written just a few days ago. I thank Darwin for making me coffee every morning, for proposing in Paris, for calling me beautiful every day, for loving me despite my flaws and craziness. I talk about how my mom loved him and how much I loved his sweet father that we lost just a few years ago. I say the words clearly and confidently, never letting my eyes leave his gaze, because I need him to hear how much I cherish him. I wipe the tears away and finish my vows with a smile on my face. I'm proud of myself for being able to speak in front of all these people that showed up for us on this important day.

The ceremony concludes and we seal it with a kiss to the applause, whistles, and shout-outs from our guests. I'm really enjoying myself! The walk back down the aisle holding hands as Mr. and Mrs. Inman was simply perfect. I see Darwin's sweet mom sitting there, and I love her so much. She is our only living parent, and I am thrilled to be her daughter-in-law; we are so very blessed. We cut the cake, drink champagne, and dance the night away. It is a glorious evening.

I keep saying "husband" and love the sound of it more and more each time I say it. I hear Darwin exclaim "my wife!" over and over, louder and louder, and it's the absolute best. He makes me laugh, and I feel so loved.

We make it back to the hotel, but not before stopping at McDonald's since Martha and I both had our fill of champagne and were too busy dancing to eat. My sister, my new husband and I are laughing the entire way from the elevator to our hotel room, where the three of us sit in our wedding clothes, on our bed that is covered in red rose pedals, eating French fries. We keep laughing until Martha leaves to go to her room, and my husband and I fall fast asleep. It's a fun ending to one of the most perfect days of my life.

Martha and I get a minute alone the next morning, and she reminds me of my hesitancy about the ceremony. "Can you believe how amazing that was? You were so nervous, and it turned into the most beautiful day." I agreed with her and felt foolish for being so anxious. I want to relive my wedding day again and again.

I tell Martha the only thing missing was Justin, and she says, "Speaking of Justin," and goes on to tell me that one of our cousin's daughters, Catherine, that is Justin's age, came up to her at the reception and asked about him.

"What did you tell her?"

"I told her the truth, and she thanked me for being honest."

I feel my heart rate jump and my face get hot and flushed. I ask her to tell me more. She explains that Catherine asked her about Justin and said, "Please Aunt Martha, no one is talking about it. No one knows what's going on, and he's my cousin. Where is Justin?" Martha then tells me that she explained to her that he had gotten involved with drugs and was struggling, but now he's in a program and doing better. I listen to my sister and I'm not exactly sure how I feel about it. I'm not mad, but I'm in compete shock. I can't believe she told her.

"Why wouldn't I tell the truth? Justin is doing good Kathy; you should be proud of him. Why are you hiding it?" Her response catches me by surprise, and it puts me in my place. I know she's right. I don't respond, and she doesn't push the subject any further. Justin is doing better, and I am proud of him. He's going to figure this out, I know he is. I don't need to hide from it anymore.

We drop Martha off, grab our bags, and head to our honeymoon in Palm Springs. Darwin filled an ice chest with drinks and snacks for us to enjoy on the ride, so I dig in. I'm in my shorts and ball cap and wearing a jersey t-shirt that says "wifey" on it. I'm a married woman! I can hardly believe it.

I put my bare feet up on the dashboard and close my eyes, listening to the song on the radio, a Bruce Springsteen song called "She's the One" that Darwin is playing for me. I love that he thinks of me when he hears this song and that he is thoughtful enough to play it.

I think about Justin who is so far away and has missed one of the most important days of my life, but I am not sad. I'm happy for him and my prayer is that someday he gets to experience this kind of love.

I want my son to live a full and meaningful life. I want him to experience joy and heartache and love so intense that it hurts sometimes. I want him to be happy and feel things—*really* feel things.

I can't wait to see the wedding pictures and send them to Justin. I want him to know that he was with me in spirit, and how grateful I am that on my wedding day, even though he was miles away, my heart was light and happy. If Justin was still on the streets, I don't know if I could have seen and felt all the love in that barn. I've gotten so good at blocking everything out that I now realize how much I've been missing.

I look over at my husband, and I'm so grateful for him. I think about Dillon's strong hand on my arm as he guided me gently down the aisle, and the look on his face when he told me I'm beautiful. I think about Justin's sweet smile that I miss so much, and I know God is looking out for us. I feel like this is a new beginning, and we have so much to look forward to.

I look down at the bouquet of yellow roses I'm still holding and I'm happy that they are still blooming and bright. I want this feeling and these beautiful yellow roses to last forever.

CHAPTER

TWENTY TWO

KATHRYN

It's back to the real world after the wedding and our honeymoon in Palm Springs. I enjoyed every single moment of my time with my new husband and kept my worries about Justin at bay. The blackout period will be over in just a few more weeks, and then I'll be able to talk to him. It's been a good and necessary break, but I'm anxious to hear how he's doing.

The Program Director calls to set up Justin's "Forgiveness Meeting" over Skype. We agree on a time, and I'm instructed to get the family together. The purpose is so Justin can take responsibility for his actions and "confess" his wrongdoings. This is a big deal because he needs to move forward. Whether or not we forgive him isn't really the issue; he just has to be able to say the words.

Dillon, Shay, Darwin, and I squeeze in together on the couch and sit looking at the fifty-inch screen TV, and we wait. Darwin is able to connect through his laptop, so we can be "live" with Justin and the director. We make the connection, and I see Justin on the screen. I'm immediately relieved. He looks good.

We make introductions, and the director leads us through the process of this meeting. He congratulates us on our recent marriage, makes small talk, and then says a prayer before we get started. Justin looks so young to me. His face is clean shaven. His hair is short, and I notice he's already gained most of his weight back. He looks nervous, and I can see that it's hard for him to sit still. I'm nervous too.

We're just ten minutes into the conversation, and we lose connection. We get it back quickly, and the director tells us it was a blessing that we had a break. Justin needed time to collect himself, and I get it! I imagine it's hard to look at the faces of the people you love and admit to all the things you did when you were in your addiction. I hope he can handle this; I hope we all can.

Justin addresses each of us one at a time; telling us what he lied about, what he stole and the things he did. He says he's sorry repeatedly. I listen to Dillon, Shay, and Darwin respond to Justin with so much love and support that I feel nothing but pride for my family. Yes, we are all broken by what we've been through. Yes, we are hurt and scared, but all that goes away if Justin can keep moving forward. We will walk this journey with him; no one is giving up.

At one point when Justin is talking to Dillon and apologizing, I can see that he's struggling with his words as the emotion rises in his voice.

"You're my brother, Dillon. I'm so sorry. I love you, and I wish I could take it all back, but I can't." Dillon thoughtfully looks at his little brother on the TV screen, as he is squirming in his seat trying to get through this, and he responds with words that bring Justin and the rest of us to tears.

"Justin, I admire you; I really do. I knew you would get through this. I love you, and I'm here for you. Whatever you need, dude. You're one of the strongest people I know. I never doubted you would get through it."

I'm not sure I've ever loved Dillon more than I do at this moment. I'm so grateful for him and my family that is sitting with me today, listening to Justin bare his soul. Despite all we've been through, they are showing Justin nothing but love and kindness.

The director tells us that at this point in our meeting he would usually talk to us about next steps and what we need to work on, but he doesn't think any of that is necessary. He praises us for being so open and loving Justin through his journey; he is impressed with our family, and honestly, I'm impressed too. I didn't know if we had anything left in us, but it turns out we have lots left for this beautiful boy who we all love so much. We say goodbye, and they disappear from the screen. Shay, Dillon, Darwin, and I all look at each other, and everyone exhales. Whew! We don't say much, but I think we are all relieved this "forgiveness meeting" is over and that Justin seems to be doing well. One day at a time.

Now that Justin has phone privileges, we're able to talk regularly. He is thriving. He's busy in Bible studies and spending time with the Lord. He's learning new trades, meeting lots of interesting people and, although he misses the California sun, he loves the outdoor life Washington offers. He describes the beauty of the water, the mountains, and the lush green terrain. He sounds happy and hopeful.

I visit him several times, and it's wonderful. We enjoy each other and it feels good; there is no tension. He seems calm and focused. I'm not worrying like I used to, and I have confidence that Justin is figuring this out. He's putting his hope in the Lord and turning to Him for guidance. I see the house he's living in, the kitchen he cooks in, the church he attends, and I get to meet the guys he's living with. This helps me when I get home after a visit because I can almost see his day and what he's doing, and that's important to me.

During our daily phone conversations, Justin and I talk a little about the future. After graduation he has no plans to come back to California. He will move to the graduation house and find a job and start his new life. It feels right.

Justin is about a month away from graduation when he calls me at work. There's a problem, and he sounds panicked; he tells me he's probably getting kicked out of the program. He's not getting along with the director, and they had a big blow up. He explains that he wants me to hear it from him first, and not from the director. His bags are packed, he's moving to Bothell, Washington. He tells me he will be fine. He'll stay in a shelter until he finds a job. "I will figure this out, Mom. I'll be fine, I promise."

I take a deep breath and close my eyes, as I'm listening to him, and I start whispering a prayer to Jesus; please give me the words to help my son; help me to guide him. I tell Justin he's got to fight to stay in the program.

"Son, remember, this has nothing to do with you and the director;

forget about him. It has everything to do with you and the Lord."
Justin is quiet; he's listening. I tell him to set his pride aside and be
humble, take responsibility, and ask for their consideration.

"Talk to them like your life depends on it because I think it does.
You must convince them to let you stay, Son. You need to finish this
program." Justin is listening, but still not responding, so I keep going.
"Okay Justin Dean, I'm going to ask you to do something for me. Give
it twenty-four hours and think about it. I mean really think and pray
about this before you decide. Please, do this for me, if not for any
other reason; just give it twenty-four hours."

It's quiet for a few more seconds, and then Justin responds.

"Okay, thanks Mom, I'll do it. I'll pray about it and let you know"
and we end our call. I find myself smiling because the Lord gave me
words, and Justin was listening. I keep praying for him to do the right
thing and stick this out because in my heart I know this is where he
needs to be.

Justin reflects and prays about it and is deeply humbled. He wants
another chance in this program, so he stays up late that night and
prepares a letter for the board of directors at The Mission House. The
next day he goes before the board and convinces them to let him stay.
His time in the program is extended by an additional three months,
and they need to see progress. Justin eagerly agrees to their terms,
and something shifts in him. This is a critical time for Justin, and it's
when God starts to completely transform his heart. Justin is given
conditions that he must follow, and he does. He's not testing the rules;
he's complying with them and setting the example for others—not
because he's forced to, but because he wants to. I hear the change in
his voice; I can hear the humility and obedience, and I am so grateful.
He's digging deep and figuring it out.

Graduation comes in May 2016. Dillon and I pack our bags and
make the trip to watch the ceremony, and it is amazing. The director
has tears in his eyes as he describes the arrogant young man that
seemed to get on his every nerve during his time in the program.
He talks about how he didn't think Justin would make it through to
graduation, and how much he's grown in the last several months. He
speaks of humility and describes Justin as a young man whose heart
has "truly been transformed in Christ." I watch my son on stage as

he accepts his certificate with nothing but hope and love in his eyes for all the good days that lie ahead of him, and I am filled with joy. I mutter a "hallelujah" under my breath as Dillon and I make our way through the crowd up to the stage to congratulate him. This is a day of celebration.

Justin opts out of the promising jobs that await him in another town and decides to stay on as manager at The Mission House. I think it's the right choice. He makes just enough to live on and has housing, a phone, and access to a car. He's in charge of the guys in the house and is stepping up to that responsibility beautifully. Things just keep getting better.

The director leaves and is replaced by a guy named Oliver, who is an amazing, godly man with a lovely wife and three beautiful young children that Justin adores. After church one day, Oliver approaches Justin.

"I'm not sure what your plans are, but I feel like we're supposed to work together; stay here!" Justin listens to him and takes his words to heart. There may be more opportunities for him in the future of this ministry.

Everything is falling into place. I'm happy in my own life, and Justin is finding his way in his. When I get a call from Justin, instead of my heart rate increasing from stress, it leaps in joyful anticipation. I'm not worried; I'm hopeful. Everything is going great until one Saturday afternoon when I fall apart.

I'm doing housework and sweeping the patio when Justin calls. He's on his way back from a job and is irritated; he says he needs to vent. I hear his voice and stomach turns, and I can feel the heavy thump of my pulse throughout my entire body. He's repeating himself. I think I hear a crack in his voice. Oh no. Please God no. My thoughts are racing. He's high again.

"Justin, are you okay? Why are you repeating yourself?"

"What? Yeah, Mom, I'm fine, what do you mean?"

"Justin, come on, what's going on? You don't sound good," and then there is silence on the phone. I tell him sharply, "Hey I have to go, I can't talk to you right now, not when you're like this." And without waiting for a response, I hang up. I try to collect myself. My heart is pounding so hard I can feel it all the way in my temples. I feel instant rage. I go upstairs to my bedroom and close the door behind me. What happens now? I try to slow my breathing.

My phone rings again, and it's Justin. He's facetiming me. I find that odd but answer anyway. I see his face fill the screen on my phone. I see his clear, brown eyes and big smile and I'm confused, but I listen.

"Hi Mom, I just wanted you to be able to see me, do you see me?"

"Yes, Son, I see you."

"Okay, keep looking at me. Make sure you *really* see me. I'm going to call you back in five minutes so pick up, okay?"

I respond "Okay," and we hang up. I sit there and think. He looked good and sounded good. Five minutes passes, and he calls me back.

"Hi Mom, how are you?"

"I'm good, Son, how are you?"

"I'm okay." Then I hear him chuckle, "I'm just working on giving you the grace you deserve and trying hard not to be insulted. Was I really repeating myself?"

Oh my gosh. He's not high! He sounds and looks perfectly fine. What just happened? I close my eyes and search for words and then apologize. "I'm so sorry, Son, it's just that you sounded weird for a minute, and I thought . . . I just . . ."

"Hey, hey, it's okay, Mom, you've been through a lot; this is going to take some time. Are you okay? You know I'm okay, right? I mean, I'm really good; I'm solid. You don't have to worry about that anymore." We say goodbye with a promise to talk later. I sit there and cry, and I'm not sure why I'm crying. Partly from relief and partly because I just feel bad. I try to get my head around what just happened. Am I that weak that at the first sign of something in his voice, I jump all the way back into desperation and fear? I remind myself where my hope lies and say a prayer asking for strength.

My mind plays a tape in my head. I'm seeing how God's hands have guided us. The times I had to handle drug dealers Justin owed money to, and they never hurt me. When Justin should have died of an overdose many times, but instead he lived. Meeting Jason that day and learning about The Mission House, the nurse in the emergency room at Kaiser that prayed for us, the counselor in Detox that prayed for Justin, the test results that came back negative, the beds that became open, the airline that welcomed him on the flight with no valid identification, and The Mission House that brought him in, and ultimately transformed him. All these visions are replaying in my head, and instead of seeing the ugliness that we went through; all I see is good. All I see is God's mercy, grace, and love that has been poured over us throughout this entire journey; His fingerprints are everywhere.

I think about how I've been consumed by Justin's addiction for the last five years and how everything and everyone else was secondary to it. My relationships, my family, my health, my well-being, my God, my everything, was secondary to Justin's addiction, and I wonder, what if I was consumed with the Lord and everything outside of Him was secondary? What would it be like if I sought Him first in all and lived only to please and glorify Him? I think about that and want it so badly.

When that feeling of desperation and fear hits me, I feel like I'm drowning and have to claw my way back to breathing again. I either run at my fears, hitting them head-on as fast as I can to conquer them, or I retreat into isolation and darkness. Each time I end up desperate and empty again. I have a choice to make; I'm either going to honor or deny God. There is no living in-between. I must choose between love and hate, darkness or light, truth or lies, and I choose truth; I choose the Lord.

I think about Justin and how well he's doing and again wonder what I would do if he relapsed. If today was a test then I failed miserably, but it has taught me something. God always uses our suffering for good. I think I'm starting to understand the depths of His love for us.

I'm reminded of my favorite scripture, Proverbs 3:5-6 (NLT) that says "Trust in the Lord with all your heart; do not depend on your own understanding. Seek his will in all you do, and he will show you which path to take." I let the scripture sink in. It is His will and not my own. I know this, and yet I still buckle to the lies that whisper in my ear saying I need control, and that I need to dive in and fight for Justin. But I don't need to fight for Justin anymore; he is the son of a mighty God that loves him more than I ever could.

CHAPTER

TWENTY THREE

KATHRYN

It's May 2016, and Justin has graduated. He's had nine clean months, and is transformed. I see it. I can hear it in his voice, but I don't exactly trust it. Not completely anyway. I can't trust it just yet because, well, we've been through this more than once. But this time does feel different, and I know that God's hands are on my son.

Justin has postponed the inevitable as long as possible; it is time to come back to California and face the music. He has to confront all the criminal charges pending against him and clean up the mess he's trying to move on from. The list of charges includes petty theft, possession of a controlled substance, possession of drug paraphernalia, and multiple parole violations. Justin has warrants in four different counties, so it's going to take a lot of restitution and phone calls to get everything cleared up. In the end, Justin realizes the best way to take care of this mess is to get on a plane back to California and simply turn himself in, so that is what he does.

Justin calls me from jail to let me know he's okay and to tell me the date and time of his court arraignment. The day finally comes; I show up an hour early and wait. I'm a bundle of nerves and praying that this goes well. The confidence I heard in Justin's voice when I talked to him is my only comfort during the week he spent in jail.

The judge takes his seat, and court is called to order. The door on the right side of the judge opens, and the inmates start to walk in. All of them are dressed in orange jumpsuits with shackles. As they start lining up, I quickly spot Justin. He looks tired but otherwise good. Clean cut and out of place. As hard as it is to see him in shackles and prison attire, I am happy to see him look so out of place.

As the men line up in front of the judge to talk about their cases, it is not going well. The judge seems like a serious, by-the-book type, and I don't sense he has much compassion. This is not good. I wait as each name is called, and it continues to go badly for each of these men. I start to get nervous. I can't imagine Justin staying in jail; it just didn't make any sense to me that he would have to serve more time. Finally, Justin is called before the judge. The judge looks him over and runs through the long list of charges pending against him and then asks, "So you've graduated from a drug program, have you?"

"Yes, your honor I have."

He continues and asks Justin a few more questions. Then the judge, in a sarcastic tone says, "I bet you think your clean cut, good looks are going to help you in this situation, don't you?"

Justin respectfully replies, "No, Your Honor." The judge seemed to reflect on Justin's response and stares at him. We sit there quietly for a few minutes waiting, and then the judge lifts his hand and slams his wrist down on the podium with surprising force. I jump in my seat.

"I have no idea why I'm doing this, and let it be known that it is against my better judgment, but I'm going to let you go today, and before you get excited, let me tell you, son, if I see you here again, I'm going to put you away for an awfully long time. Do you understand me?" The judge is practically yelling. Justin's face is flush, and I know he's rattled, but much to his credit, he stays composed and responds, "I understand, Your Honor, thank you, sir," and that was it. On his way out of the courtroom, Justin turns around and gives me a quick smile. We are both flooded with relief.

Wearing an orange jumpsuit, with shackles around his wrists and ankles, Justin exits the courtroom to go back to jail and sit in the holding tank until his release. I head to my car and try to process what just happened. Today was unnerving, but the outcome was good. Justin will be released and fly back to his life in Washington. Praise God.

Justin gets settled back in Washington, and a few months later receives a "check in" court date in the mail and, after a few phone calls, is told that he must show up in person. It's tough to manage because he is working, but he figures it out and flies back to California just for one day. Justin arrives, and we drive together to court in Fremont, bright and early on a Thursday. Justin has his completion certificate and reference letter from The Mission House in hand, and he looks good. He's clean-shaven and is dressed in a crisp, white collared shirt, and slacks. He looks like a strong, healthy young man, with no visible evidence of the life he was living less than a year ago.

Justin has been corresponding with the courts and was under the impression that this court date was standard protocol as a probation check; he assures me that there is nothing to be concerned about. He served his week in jail and has slowly been paying off his restitution, so this seemed like a mere formality. He has a return flight booked so he can head back to Washington that same evening.

Justin is assigned a Public Defender (PD) who talks with him briefly. She explains that the District Attorney (DA) is tough, but that she would do her best to help. I'm thinking, whoa, hold on a minute, what does that mean? So, we wait, and wait, and wait, and I wonder why it's taking so long. Finally, his name is called, and Justin goes before the judge. The judge starts reading off the same long list of offenses, many of which Justin doesn't even remember. He's told he can never enter a Toys-R-Us, Target, or Rite-Aid again. Justin, looking confused, says he will stay away from those stores. The Public Defender talks privately with the District Attorney, and they approach the bench and talk to the judge. We're waiting, Justin standing, me sitting, both of us getting increasingly nervous, and then they move on to the next case. We are confused and not sure what is happening. Our Public Defender, a kind, beautiful woman, with curly brown hair, approaches us and says the District Attorney wants Justin to serve six months in jail for his laundry list of offenses, and she won't entertain any kind of plea bargain. I am in shock. The color from Justin's face drains. The PD asks Justin, "Can you wait for a while? I'm not done yet. Let me see what else I can do." Justin nods, calmly says, "Of course," and we sit. I turn to Justin and start to speak; he shakes his head no. I stop. We can't talk right now, there is nothing to say, so I start praying silently, and I'm guessing Justin is doing the same.

Our PD walks a few steps towards us and then waves Justin down to accompany her in the hallway. Justin walks down the stairs to her, and I see them start talking as they are walking away. I hear her say, "I've never done this before, Justin, but can you do me a favor?

That's all I needed to hear. I can feel Jesus at work in this courtroom, and I'm instantly filled with relief knowing that somehow this is going to work out. Turns out the favor involved a case where an 18-year-old boy and his mom were in the courthouse that day. He was a drug user and spiraling out of control quickly. The kid's mom is devastated, and the PD wants Justin to talk with them. He enters a counseling room and does his best to speak truth into the kid and support the mom. They ask for his card, and Justin gives it to them. They return to their seats in front of us, and I see the young man slip Justin's card in his wallet.

Our PD is talking to the DA again, and we see her look up in our direction. Then our PD approaches us and tells us that she is asking the DA to talk to Justin, to sit with him so she can actually see him. She says, "I think if you can get in front of her, she may reconsider." Our PD leaves, and we remain seated in silence. More time passes and I start to wonder if we need to change Justin's flight. We hear the DA tell the judge, in an annoyed voice, "For some reason she wants me to talk to Mr. Usiak, so let's get him down here."

Justin walks through the rows of courthouse seats, past the bailiff, through the gate and sits down in the chair next to the DA. I'm watching and cannot read her face; she's showing no emotion. After about five minutes of them talking, Justin returns to his seat. I ask him how it went, and he tells me he has no idea, he just told her the truth about his past and where he is now and thanked her for any consideration. We continue waiting. Our PD reappears, and Justin gets called up to stand before the judge. They once again start reading off the offenses, and the judge calculates the fines; the DA says, "Let's waive the fines, Your Honor." The Judge brings up jail time; the DA tells him, "Please waive the jail time and replace it with community service, Your Honor."

The judge states, "Mr. Usiak lives in Washington." The DA replies, "Let's include that he can do his community service in Washington

State, Your Honor." They continue with this for a while, and then everyone returns to their seats and starts gathering their papers; it appears we are finally done. We walk out of there with Justin assigned forty hours of community service to be served in Washington, and two years informal probation.

We walk in silence out of the courtroom to the parking lot; we get in the car and just sit there for a few minutes, both of us trying to process what just happened. I can't hold back my tears any longer, and I notice Justin is emotional too. We are so overwhelmed that it's hard to speak; we're both at a total loss for words. God's mercy was raining down on us in that courtroom. The Lord is at work! I've never witnessed anything quite like this in my life. Justin hears a beep on his phone and reads an email from the PD. She is praising Justin for the hard work he is doing in his life, encouraging him to continue moving forward, and asks if she can refer young people that are struggling to him for help. She includes Justin's mug shots and writes, "If you ever feel tempted to go back to your old life; look at these photos; these don't look like the man I saw today. You take good care of yourself, and please keep in touch." Justin wrote her back immediately, thanking her for everything. We set off for the airport and arrive on time. We say goodbye with a promise to talk when he lands.

As I watch him leave, I flash back on the young, thin, nervous boy, we put on a plane just over a year ago. Justin is becoming the man I believe God intended him to be. His heart is transformed, my heart is transformed, and I believe it with everything in me.

CHAPTER

TWENTY FOUR

KATHRYN

It's 5:10 p.m. and I just got off work. I pull into the garage, turn off the house alarm, kick off my heels, and dash into my bedroom. I step out of my skirt, pull off my blouse and rummage around my closet to find my worn-out jeans, oversized sweater, and slip-on comfy shoes. I brush my teeth, throw my hair into a ponytail, take a glance in the mirror, and do a quick inventory: keys, phone, purse, check! I hop in my Jeep and head back out.

As I drive across town, my heart is already warming in anticipation of meeting Valerie and Kristen, my warrior sisters. We have been through it in our lives; I mean we have *really* been through some stuff. Pain, suffering, and addiction initially brought us together, but it is love, hope and sisterhood that bind us.

Our bond is strong, and I expect that we will be lifelong friends. We have an unspoken agreement that when one of us reaches out, the others will respond. We answer the text message or phone call; we check in on each other when we haven't talked in a while, and we pray; we pray for each other, and we pray for our families.

We lift each other up and laugh, despite the pain. They say that laughter is good medicine, and to that I say amen, amen, amen.

We have a lot in common. The three of us are within five years of each other in age; we're all married; we're believers; we raised our families, had our careers, live in Modesto—and we have sons who are addicts. Combined we have a total of seven biological kids; four of whom have struggled in addiction. At some point before we met, all four of our sons were homeless, in jail, in rehabs, addicted to heroin, addicted to meth, alcohol, or whatever their drug of choice was. They've been clean and then relapsed, and in and out of multiple programs. They've lied to us and done all the things that people deep in addiction often do. These beloved young men that we've loved and raised, each so beautiful and unique, have led us on paths that are more similar than different.

Sometimes all four are doing well; sometimes there is relapse; often there are extra prayers for the ones that are still lost in the dark pits of addiction. No matter what the circumstances are, we don't allow each other to give up.

As I pull into the restaurant parking lot, I see Valerie's ice-blue Honda parked in front. She's a schoolteacher and probably the sweetest person I've ever met. I open the door to the restaurant and feel the smile cross my lips, because I know in just a few seconds I'll be wrapped in her arms, and she will look at me and ask how I am. Her eyes will search mine because she is checking on me; she genuinely wants to know how I am, and I love that. As I'm walking into the restaurant, my mind drifts back to when and how we first met.

Justin was in The Mission House and had just finished his forty-five-day blackout period. It's late in the afternoon, and I walk back into my office after a grueling three-hour meeting with our leadership team. I hear my phone buzzing and see that it's Justin. I quickly answer, excited to talk to my son who is safe and sober in Washington state while I'm safe and somewhat sane in the California. His voice sounds good. He explains that he doesn't have long to talk but wanted to tell me about a graduation he went to at a local faith-based program that's much like The Mission House. At the graduation he learned that one of the graduates was from Modesto. He listened to the testimony of the kid that graduated and said his mom spoke as well, and that she reminded him of me.

He goes on to describe how this mom was relentless in helping her son; she kept calling, trying to get him in the program, and when they didn't call her back right away, she just continued to call and left a message saying, "You better pick up the phone, because I will keep calling all night long if I have to." The crowd at the graduation laughed at this, and Justin laughed too, but it wasn't just the laughter that caught his attention. Through the stories and testimony of this mother and son, he caught a glimpse of the love they shared, and it reminded him of our journey.

Justin tells me that after the ceremony he introduced himself to the mom (Valerie) and son (Zak), and they connected immediately. They soon discovered that Zak and Justin were just a few years apart and had mutual friends. Justin also learned that Valerie went to the same church that I was attending.

Justin goes on to say that he gave her my phone number and asked her to call me so we could get together. It was quiet on the phone as I'm realizing Justin is expecting me to actually talk to and meet up with this mom if and when she decides to call me. I understand his intention, but I'm wondering what I would say to her. I'm an introvert, and he knows this. I don't want any new friends, thank you very much. The last thing I want to do is to connect with a mom who has lived in the misery of addiction. I mean, come on! What is the point? Did he expect us to share horror stories over a tuna sandwich? Or compare heartache while sipping a Mocha Frappuccino at the local Starbucks? I take a deep breath that I'm sure he can hear, and exhale slowly, silently wondering what in the world my son was thinking.

As if reading my mind, in a calm and gentle voice Justin says "Mom, just please take her call. You will love her, I promise. You need this kind of support. Trust me on this, Mom! Take ... the ... call ..." He was pushing hard, so I tried to sound enthusiastic and assured him I would take the call, even though I was certain that I wouldn't.

A few days later I'm working at my desk and hear my phone buzzing. I glance at it, don't recognize the number, so I let it keep ringing and ignore it. My heart rate always goes up when my phone shows a number I don't recognize. My first thought is it's for sure bad news; my second thought is that it's about Justin. Old habits do die hard. Even though Justin was safe in a program 820 miles away, I had the same old reaction—I still had healing to do.

Later that evening as I'm driving home from work, I remember the call and see that I have a voice mail. I listen to this mom Justin gave my number to go into a long explanation that sounded something like "Hi, it's Val, you don't know me, but your son gave me your phone number, ha ha ha. I'm just now realizing this may sound weird, but hopefully he told you I would be calling. Anyway, I met him in Washington. He is an absolute delight, . . ." and she continued on, ending with "Call me." I found myself smiling at her message and Justin's voice is ringing in my ear, "Just talk to her, Mom, you need support." I mull it over; she has a son that just graduated, and she survived the nightmare. Before I let myself overthink it too much, I pull my Jeep over to the side of the road and call her back.

We talk, and it's good. In our first conversation, she quickly let me know how strong and healthy Justin looks and what a handsome young man she thinks he is. A little part of me relaxes hearing that information, and then I'm intrigued by her. She knew I needed to hear that first, before I could listen to anything else. She totally gets it. When you have a child battling addiction you find yourself constantly assessing their appearance. Do his eyes look clear? Does his voice sound strong? Does he look pale? Is he losing weight? It's maddening when you're always looking for a sign of relapse, as much as I hated it, I just couldn't seem to stop myself. Anyway, our conversations continue, and I find them easy. I'm surprised by how comfortable I am with her.

The next week I go to Wednesday night service at church and get to meet her and her husband in person. After introductions, Valerie and I immediately embrace. My heart fills with emotion at the connection I already feel. Valerie's husband gives me a huge hug and tells me what a pleasure it was to meet my son. These are good people.

Valerie has fought the battle; she loves her son as much as I love mine, and she has lived through the nightmare. She is pretty and confident, and she's not wearing her pain like I do—and that makes me curious. Over the next several months, we meet for coffee, a glass of wine or dinner, and we talk for hours, and it's good. Surprisingly healing.

I tell Justin about our growing friendship, and he praises me, "Keep going, Mom, this is what you need!" I couldn't help but marvel at his newfound wisdom about what I need. The thought makes me laugh. Justin giving me advice? Who would have guessed! But he was right, her friendship already feels important.

Before I knew it, months have passed, and now there are four of us meeting for dinner. The group includes Katy, who I would describe as a kind and spiritual warrior. She's calm and positive; it was amazing just to be in her presence. She is the only one with a daughter that had been on the street for about eight years with no end to her troubles in sight; she had never even tried a program. I listen to her describe the heartache, and for once I feel fortunate. As bad as it was having Justin on the street, I could not imagine what it would be like to have a daughter out there. Katy's daughter was involved in an accident, and they eventually both moved away, but I still think of her from time to time.

Also in the group was Kristen, a spitfire who is small in stature, and stunning in her beauty. Kristen has two sons that have struggled in addiction. She, like Valerie, had a confidence about her, and I saw no trace of the pain I knew she'd endured.

My walk-in faith is strengthened through knowing these women, and we developed a strong friendship. It's more like a sisterhood, and I cherish it. We made it a point to meet at least monthly for dinner and, oddly, I never cancel; I always look forward to our time together.

As the bell on the door sounds, I see Valerie in the restaurant sitting at a booth. Her dark hair drapes beautifully on her shoulders, and she looks in my direction. Her sea green eyes are already smiling as she sees me walk in. As expected, she stands, and we greet each other as if it's been years; it's always like that. We hear the bell again and see Kristen making her way to us, and the embracing continues.

We take our seats and start talking, and the waitress interrupts us; we order water with lemon and decide on drinks. I order the Sauvignon Blanc, my favorite white wine. Valerie orders the sweetest wine on the menu, and Kristen, after a couple of questions for the waitress, decides on a beer. We look at menus and then get caught up in our conversation only to be interrupted by the waitress again. We laugh and ask for a few more minutes. Eventually I order the salad with fish; Valerie gets the General Tsao, and Kristen, after much deliberation and a few more questions for the waitress, decides on the Pad Thai. We're three girls excited about getting a drink, eager to eat something off the menu, and loving our time together. We join hands, and Kristen leads us in prayer, thanking the Lord for our time together and blessings for our food.

With food and drinks ordered and prayers made, we dive into conversation. Each of us take turns updating each other on the latest in our lives and how our sons are doing. We listen attentively and don't interrupt; always good, always comforting. We gulp down our drinks and devour our food between sentences and notice that a few hours have already passed. We gather our things, split the tab, and with a hug and I love you, we part ways, already planning our next date.

Over our dinner conversations, they've heard it all from me. I've shared my story with all the gory details, and they never flinched. They never judge me; they just keep loving and lifting me up. I've showed them my scars; they've heard my pain, they've seen and shared in my heartache, and they've loved me through it. And they've shared with me; stories equally as bad—just different. The relief and comfort I feel from our shared journeys astounds me. Martha kept telling me to seek support. "Find people that understand what you've been through, get in a small group." She must have told me this dozens of times, and now I get it. This is what Martha was talking about; this is what she knew I needed.

Each night we meet for dinner is typically followed up by a group text saying how much fun we had and how grateful we are to have each other. I always leave feeling better than when I got there.

I pull in my driveway and have to fumble to get in the door because it's dark. I guess I forgot to turn the porch light on. I turn the key, open the door, go to turn off the alarm, and then realize I never set it. I flop down on the couch and think about that call from Justin several years ago when he encouraged me to connect with Valerie. I'm so thankful. My son nudged me to take a chance on someone, and it turned into something beautiful. How great is that?

I start getting ready for bed. I wash my face, brush my teeth, pile my hair up in a bun and stop to look at myself in the mirror, assessing my reflection. My pain isn't as visible as it used to be. I know that everything could fall apart tomorrow, or next month, or next year even, but that is not my concern today.

I take a long, deep, and cleansing breath, throw my clothes in the pile collecting in the corner, and crawl in my warm, safe bed. Darwin is out of town on business, so the house is empty and quiet; the only sound is the white clock tick-tocking in the living room. I don't feel like reading tonight. I turn off the light, thank Jesus for his love, wrap myself in the warmth of my bed, and close my eyes.

Sleep does not come, as I lie there thinking about my day. I think about how I forgot to set the house alarm this evening and didn't turn on the porch light. I ponder the pile of dirty clothes and towels forming in the corner of my room and the bed I just slid into that was not made. I turn the light back on and sit up looking around, somehow surprised by this discovery. The house wasn't in perfect order today; I forgot some of the things I normally do, the daily rituals that make me feel in control of my environment. This is not like me. I'm feeling some pride in the realization that I'm loosening up a bit. I say out loud to no one at all "Good job, Kathryn Mae, look at you spending time with friends and leaving your house a mess, that's so awesome."

I turn the light back off and nestle beneath the covers. I'm comforted by my progress. I'm feeling loved and strong.

ALL I NEED

CHAPTER

TWENTY FIVE

JUSTIN JANUARY 2017

As I reflect on my life, I don't know how I survived. I take that back; I know exactly how I made it. God saved me; He freed and delivered me. It's like He reached down from the heavens and pulled me out of the grave. I know I should be dead, but I've been given another chance, and I am so grateful. Saying I'm grateful is the understatement of the century, but I just can't seem to find the right words to explain how happy I am. I have been redeemed and made new in Christ.

This morning I woke up from a sound sleep just before 5:00 a.m. I start my day with a hot shower; I take them daily now, sometimes twice a day. I pull a clean t-shirt, a pair of boxers and socks out of my dresser where they are neatly folded. I grab my jeans and a flannel shirt from my closet, get dressed and ready for another day in the great Northwest. I shave, brush my teeth, make my bed, and head to the kitchen for my first cup of coffee with lots of cream. I turn on the lamp at my desk, open my Bible and begin my morning study of His word.

I am learning, I mean *really learning,* for the first time in a long time. I'm hungry for truth and want to soak in as much as I can about Christ and how to live an honorable life. So many things that I used to believe are just not true; like what it means to be a man. A strong man is someone who loves others, is kind, humble, forgiving, and patient. I used to think being a man was about physical strength and possessions, but those things do not represent happiness. True happiness comes from the heart. I have finally found what I've been chasing my entire life; the peace and contentment that comes from knowing Christ.

God really transformed me after I almost got kicked out of The Mission House. I was packed and ready. So, I called my mom to let her know I had to leave the program, and then she said the right thing at the exact right time "Son, remember, this has nothing to do with you and the director; forget about him. It has everything to do with you and the Lord." It was only then that I dug deep and, by the grace of God, convinced them to let me stay. From there I began to understand obedience, humility, and how to really love others. I've never looked back.

Now I see the world and the people in it with new eyes. The man I want to be is gentle, kind, and loving. The change in me really hit home when I had to go serve a week in jail back in California. When I was in my addiction, I was always comfortable in jail, because the prison yard "dog eat dog" mentality wasn't much different than the streets of Oakland. But this time when I turned myself in and went to jail, I felt like a scared little kid. I laid in my bunk gripping my Bible while inmates in my block gathered around right next to me, listening to rap music, and snorting meth all night long. I kept trippin' on the fact that not too long ago I was one of them, but now I'm not. I wanted nothing to do with drugs, and I felt out of place. I was terrified.

I did not deserve another chance, but I got one, and I'm not going to blow it. The Lord has granted me a life worth living, and I'm grabbing hold of it with everything in me.

I have a little money in the bank, and I'm slowly paying off my debts. I've got some food in the refrigerator and a warm bed to sleep in at night. I'm telling you, you really appreciate every little thing when you've lived with absolutely nothing. The level of depravity that I was living in is hard to imagine if you haven't been there. Drugs were the only thing that helped me numb myself, but now I don't want to be numb; I want to feel everything. There's not a day that passes that

I don't find myself choking back tears, because I'm so grateful for a clear mind, a healthy body, and a chance at a new life.

I have a hard time wrapping my head around the fact that it hasn't even been two years since I was strung out and homeless. Back then I couldn't go three hours without drugs or I would be sick, but now I'm healthy and active. Today all my cravings are gone. I have no urges or "needs" to fill. I'm not fighting them or working on them; they simply don't exist. I don't touch alcohol, tobacco, or drugs. I don't consume energy drinks, and my language is cleaned up; you won't hear me use profanity. I know I'm always one bad decision away from self-destruction, but for today, I am blessed because God has made me new. Man, it feels so good to be good again.

My body is healing; I've gained my weight back, and I feel strong. I can still see scars on my legs from picking my skin, and the track marks are still there, but they've faded. I think my veins are slowly repairing themselves because when I had to get a blood test recently, they were able to find a vein pretty quickly. Thank you, God, for healing. My last dentist appointment went surprisingly well. Despite the way I was living, I didn't even have a cavity. It's so crazy! I was using heavily and had no nutrition whatsoever, but somehow, I walked away without any diseases or permanent damage, other than the scars on my skin. In a way I'm glad they're there, it serves as a daily reminder of the past and how far I've come since God rescued me.

My relationship with my family is on the mend. I realize how blessed I am to have such kind and loving people in my corner. I know it will take some time for them to heal and really trust me again, but I will do everything I can to make them proud. I can't tell you how good it feels to call my brother and just shoot the breeze, or when I call my lifelong friend, Cody, and we laugh about old times, and the sound of my mom's voice when we talk; she's always excited to hear every single detail of my day. I feel like I have literally come back from the dead.

I'm not planning my life too far in advance. I find that I'm better off living each day, doing the best I can and staying in prayer, so my eyes are wide open, and my decisions are sound. I have mentors, accountability partners, and a community of brothers-in-Christ that lift me up and support me, and I've grown to depend on them.

On my days off, I often go for a run or hike in the mountains or fishing with a buddy. I love nature; when I'm in it I feel like all my senses are heightened. When the weather is nice and the sky is clear, you can see Mount Rainier, the highest mountain on the Cascade Range in Washington. I could stare at that great mountain for hours; just stand there staring, in awe of its massive beauty. I find myself breathing deeply, trying to let the wonder of it fill every one of my senses. I pray a lot when I'm in nature because that's where I feel closest to God.

I'm driving home in our company truck after a long day of work. I have the music turned up loud when a song comes on that takes my breath away. I want to focus on the song, so I pull over to the side of the road. I close my eyes and listen to the lyrics, and I'm suddenly overcome with a rush of emotion...

> *Alone in my sorrow and dead in my sin*
> *Lost without hope and no place to begin*
> *Your love made a way to let mercy come in*
> *When death was arrested, and my life began*
> *Ash was redeemed only beauty remains*
> *My orphan heart was given a name*
> *My mourning grew quiet my feet rose to dance*
> *When death was arrested, and my life began*
> *Oh, your grace so free*
> *Washes over me*
> *You have made me new*
> *Now life begins with You*
> *It's your endless love*
> *Pouring down on us*
> *You have made us new*
> *Now Life begins with You*
> *Released from my chains I'm a prisoner no more*
> *My shame was a ransom He faithfully bore*
> *He canceled my debt and He called me His friend*
> *When death was arrested, and my life began*

Song by North Point- InsideOut (Death Was Arrested)

I stayed there, parked on the side of the road, long after the song ended. It was a cold and gloomy day. The sky was dark gray and the wind was blowing, so you could feel the chill deep in your bones, but it felt good to me. I just sat there in my truck with the windows down and my head resting on the steering wheel; I didn't even bother wiping my tears away; I just let them flow. I've done so many bad things in my life, things I should never be forgiven for, but God has forgiven all. My family still loves me; I am healthy, and I'm so grateful. I know my loved ones are happy to see the physical changes in me, because they are obvious, but the biggest change is on the inside; God has changed and filled my heart.

I will never forget how bad things were, but I will not let it weigh me down. I will shake off the burdens of the past and live every day loving life and the people in it with my whole heart, and I will spend every waking hour praising the God that saved me, because He is all that matters.

I don't have things figured out yet. I don't know how to budget my money; I don't know how to date as a godly man, and I'm not sure what my future holds, but that's okay, because I know the Lord will guide my steps.

Despite all the pain and suffering, the rehabs, my recovery, my past, and all the uncertainties in this life, all I need is Christ. His word tells me I am a son of God; I am His beloved, and I am forgiven. If I keep my eyes fixed on Christ, I will be fine. He has shown me that He is sovereign and faithful. Even at my darkest, He kept pursuing me, because He loves me more than I could ever love myself. No matter what I face in the days to come, I know one thing for certain, and I believe it with every ounce of me; Christ is all I need. He is now, and will forever be, enough.

CHAPTER

TWENTY SIX

KATHRYN

Justin continues to grow in his ministry and is becoming exactly the man I believe God intended him to be. He is thriving in his work and recently was promoted to the position of Associate Director of The Mission House, working under Oliver, who has become one of his best friends and brother-in-Christ. Justin and Oliver make an incredible team. Justin is growing in his walk and is trusting and seeking Christ in all aspects of life. Justin's increase in responsibilities was the boost he needed to pursue his certification in biblical counseling. He's becoming a strong leader and has a gift for walking alongside the men entering the program. Justin is planting seeds of hope and leading men to Christ. With the increase in responsibilities came an increase in his monetary compensation, and he is encouraged by that.

Justin is surrounded by a community of believers and has made some good friends. He is happy, healthy, and he is ready for a relationship. Justin tells me he needs to find a wife! I remember one conversation, when he mentions that all his friends are married with strong women by their side, and he wants that. He wants a wife, a house full of kids, and a dog. I laugh at him, and feel overjoyed with the goals he's setting, and I am absolutely certain that he will find everything he's looking for.

A beauty named Amanda is on his radar. She is a senior in college and is currently in Israel on a mission trip. He heard from a good friend and others in the community that she is his "perfect match," which is intriguing to him. Justin looks Amanda up on social media and wonders if she could be the one. He's wondering this before he's even met her, which I find amusing. He initiates a conversation with her, and they begin messaging each other on Facebook. She is coming home to Washington for the holidays, so they make plans to meet.

She is young, beautiful, educated, strong, and she loves the Lord. She is unlike anyone he's ever dated before. I know that my son's love life is not my business, but I'm eager to hear how things go and know that Justin will keep me posted.

They meet, and he is taken by her. He wants to pursue her, so he does; trying his best to do everything right. The holidays pass, and she returns to school in Southern California, and they stay in contact with each other. He flies down to visit her, sends flowers, and reminds her to take care of herself as she is buried in studies and busy completing her finals. She graduates and moves back to Washington, and they continue seeing each other.

He is deliberate in his steps to win her heart. He prays for guidance; he is gentle, loving, and respectful to her. I marvel at the gentleman he is. He tells me about her heart and her beautiful spirit and, as I listen to him, I realize he's falling in love.

One morning as I'm headed to work, Justin calls and tells me he needs my help with something. I hear the excitement in his voice, so I pull over to the side of the road and listen as he asks me to help him figure out how to propose to Amanda. I ask if he's sure, and he tells me that God has given him conviction; she is the one he's been praying for. He is certain. He exclaims, "I love her, Mom!" and I'm thrilled for him. I hang up the phone and stay on the side of the road for a few moments, thinking about our conversation. This is all happening so fast, and I wonder if he is ready. I look up and know that God is working. My trust is in Him. He is the one leading Justin, not me. I exhale slowly trying to let myself enjoy this moment. My son is getting married!

He picks out a ring and plans the proposal in a beautiful setting by the water on the 4th of July. Fireworks were in the sky and in the hearts of these two young lovebirds on that day. She said yes!

They set the wedding date for just six weeks after the engagement on August 27, 2017. The date lingers on my mind for a few days, and then I remember; that is the date Justin got clean. His 2-year anniversary of sobriety will be on his wedding day. Wow, things have changed. I rarely even think of the dark times anymore. It seems so far away—like a distant memory from another lifetime.

The wedding day comes, and it is a sight to see. The venue is on top of a hill overlooking a country setting in Poulsbo, Washington. There are flowers and greenery everywhere and an old, charming, black and white farmhouse that sits sturdily alongside the dirt road. There are horses grazing in a pasture lined with a white fence, and it is breathtaking. The birds are singing, the sun is shining, and there is a warm breeze that rustles the leaves on the branches of the big trees that seem to frame this magical day.

Friends and family are gathered to witness the joining of these two lives. The ceremony is one of the most God-honoring, spiritual moments I've ever witnessed. Their vows are beautiful; Amanda is radiant, and my son has never looked so handsome. He looks at Amanda with such love in his eyes that my heart is overflowing for them.

I think about God's perfect timing. I think about how He has used all our struggles and suffering to bring us to this place of joy and love in abundance. The lightness I feel is indescribable. It has made its way through every fiber of my being, and I recognize that Justin isn't the only one who has been redeemed. I am made new in Christ; His spirit is within me. A wave of emotion washes over me, and I don't try to fight it, I welcome it.

I look at Justin and see how happy he is. He is settled, in love, and committed to this new life in Christ, with a strong woman by his side. The ring on his finger looks natural, and the confidence he's already showing in his role as a husband suits him.

A few months later, I receive a FaceTime call from Justin. I answer and see Justin's face fill the screen with Amanda sitting next to him; their smiles are radiant, and I know they have news. They. Are. Pregnant! I scream in excitement and can't manage to put any words together. What is happening? How is this possible? They got pregnant on their honeymoon! My mind is swirling with thoughts of a grandchild, and I am overwhelmed by God's love. He has brought our family through so much, and now we're expecting a grandchild. The blessings just keep coming, and I am praising Jesus with every breath.

The months pass slowly, as the little one is growing. There is movement, with tiny elbows rolling across Amanda's belly, and the occasional jab of a foot underneath her skin. Amanda sends videos and gives us updates after each doctor's appointment. There is excitement and the normal worries that come with having your first child. Pregnancy agrees with Amanda; she looks stunning.

The prenatal care is going well, and the baby's heartbeat is strong. Justin is excited, but I get the impression that he hasn't quite come to grips with the fact that this is actually happening. I dig through baby pictures of my children and remember when they were tiny. I become overwhelmed and filled with emotions as I turn the pages of Justin's scrap book. Will their baby look like Justin, or have Amanda's beautiful blue eyes? There is so much to look forward to; I can barely keep up.

My husband is thrilled at the thought of becoming a grandpa, and Justin's brothers and sisters are all excited about their upcoming roles as aunts and uncles. I'm excited as well, but I feel a little fragile, and I'm not sure why. Am I guarding my heart, afraid that something might happen? Am I trusting in the Lord? Or am I letting the past keep its grip on me? I decide it's probably a mix of everything, so I will myself to pray more and worry less. So much is changing, and so many good things are happening; it's a lot to take in, but I take it in, and I let the joy fill me.

Amanda and Justin are planning a gender reveal party. The date is set, so Martha and I book our flights. Martha is convinced it's a girl and is constantly sending me pictures of what she thinks this sweet little baby might look like. I look at the pictures she sends me and have no idea what to think. It could be a girl, but in my heart I'm fairly certain it will be a boy. A little soldier that Justin will teach to be a good man. He will love the Lord, respect his mom, cut wood, swing a bat, and be a gentleman. Boys are familiar and easy. When I close my eyes, I can picture Justin with his son riding high on his shoulders and it is the sweetest thing. And, what if it's a girl? A little girl would burst my heart wide open; I try to picture it and I can't. I imagine the purity of the love between a father and daughter, and it's just beautiful. I tell myself to stop thinking about the gender; we will know soon enough! The date of the gender reveal party finally comes, so Martha and I pack our bags, board the plane and head to Washington. Martha talks nonstop the entire flight about the little girl she is certain we're having. I'm excited and nervous at the same time.

Justin picks us up from the airport, and we hug tightly. He looks great and I realize how much I miss him. I look into his eyes and see the confidence of a grown man that is making moves in this world. I love him so much.

Martha and I check into our hotel and are happy to have the entire next day to hang out with Justin and Amanda and enjoy our time in beautiful Washington. I get a chance to talk with Justin alone and ask how he's doing, and he seems good. He's both nervous and excited about finding out their child's gender. He tells me how he would raise a son to be respectful and love the Lord. He talks about how he will teach him everything he knows and that he would grow up to be an honorable man. I notice the smile on Justin's face, and it's endearing; I get the sense he has thought a lot about having a son. And then Justin pauses and seems to stumble on his words, he leans in towards me, his voice just above a whisper,

"But Mom, I mean, I've thought about this and.... what if it's a girl? I'm not sure what I'll do. All I know is that I will cherish her, that's all I've got." It was a sweet moment, and I was struck by the tenderness in his voice. I look at him and understand completely because I've had some of those same thoughts. I tell him how proud I am of him and that he will be an amazing dad, and I mean it sincerely. God has given me new eyes to see my son. There is no worry or anxiety. I know, without a doubt, that he will be an incredible father.

We part ways, and Martha and I head back to our hotel to rest a bit before the party. My mind drifts, recapping the last few years. We walked out of the darkness and landed in the light with a warmth and peace so comforting that we've never looked back. Justin is helping others to heal and working with men who are in bondage. He's speaking truth into their hearts and leading them to salvation. He is a married man and soon-to-be father. Since the wedding there has been a stirring in Dillon's heart; he is asking questions and seeking the Lord, and he has found the love of his life. Dillon and Jess have been together for a few years now, and soon he will ask her to be his wife. Things just keep getting better.

I'm on my knees every morning, not crying out in agony but crying in grateful praise to the Lord for His goodness and the blessings He is pouring down on our family. There is no more darkness; there is only light. Thank you, Jesus.

The sun starts to set, so Martha and I eagerly hop on the ferry and head to Port Orchard where Justin and Amanda are waiting for us. We drive to their house which is a cute cottage with a spectacular view of the Puget Sound. We sit in their neat little home and visit for a while. As the clock ticks, I'm getting more and more nervous, and I sense that Justin is too. Martha is oozing with anticipation, and Amanda just keeps snacking because she is hungry. This makes us all laugh. She is a darling pregnant mother-to-be. It's time to go, so we all load into the car and drive up the hill to Amanda's mother, Lena's house.

It's a beautiful old farmhouse centered on a large piece of property surrounded by tall trees and lush green grass. The house is decorated with white sparkling lights, and blue and pink ribbons are everywhere. Introductions are made, and it feels good to be there for Justin and to meet these people that have come to know and love him. I watch as he interacts with his new friends and family, and I'm impressed. He is cared for, trusted by these people, and has a strong presence about him. My eyes try to capture these beautiful moments, trying to save them somehow so I can look at them again and again.

Snacks are served; punch and tea are poured, and there is a buzz of excitement in the air; this is a special day!

Amanda's lifelong friend, Meg, is in charge and lets us know the time has come, "Everyone take a seat and let's get to it!" My heart is pounding, and my hands are clammy. I look at Justin, and he looks a little rattled.

Meg brings out three black helium balloons and hands them to Justin and Amanda, along with a pin. The instructions are that on the count of three, Justin and Amanda are to pop the balloons and the gender will be revealed: pink for a girl and blue for a boy. Simple enough.

Meg stands back; Amanda and Justin are at the front of the room, and everyone is seated around them. Meg counts, 1, 2, and then both Justin and I yell, "Whoa!" at the same time, our hands outstretched as if we're trying to stop time. We are not ready!

Justin tries to compose himself and asks for instructions again. Meg explains, speaking slowly and looking directly at Justin. "I'm going to count to three, and then you're going to pop these balloons with the pin I gave you, and then we're going to find out the gender of your sweet baby." She pauses, giving Justin the time he clearly needs, and then asks, "Are you ready?" Justin takes a long, deep breath, closes his eyes for just a moment and then nods, he is ready.

I've stopped breathing entirely, Amanda's eyes are full of excitement, and Martha is bouncing up and down in her seat. Justin and I meet eyes for a split second, tears already forming and starting to fall down my face. The counting begins again, One! Two! Threeeeee! POP! The confetti bursts out of the balloons and gently falls across the room. It feels like everything is in slow motion as the flakes land on Justin and Amanda. Everyone is on their feet, jumping up and down, screaming with excitement, smiling, and clapping with joy.

I search for Justin and see his face; he's covered in confetti and his cheeks are flushed with color. His eyebrows are raised in surprise, and I can almost see his heart exploding out of his chest. All the love and light in the room seems to have gathered to rest in Justin's eyes that are glistening with tears. He looks frozen in place as he gazes up at the confetti that continues falling; the beautiful bright pink confetti that gives us a glimpse of the sweet little baby that will be cherished by her daddy for all her days; it's a girl!

THE END

NEVER LOST AGAIN

As I suffered and hid in the dark
You were there, I just didn't know it;
When I screamed and cursed all that was lost,
You were waiting for me to see You.

When there was no light, only darkness,
You protected my heart with your love,
And when I was empty and helpless to fight,
You fought for me because it was never my battle.

When I was destroyed and couldn't find my voice,
You spoke life back into my soul,
And when I couldn't feel the sun,
You stirred the warmth back in and let it fill me.

When I finally cried out and surrendered,
You were there waiting, wrapping me in your grace and mercy.
Now I see You, I feel You, I turn to You;
With every step and breath, I seek You.

I see the sweet beauty in the works of your hands.
Your love and power wash over me.
In your light and love I will stand,
Never to be lost again.

Kathryn Mae Inman

EPILOGUE

Our story was a rough one; it's intense and filled with gut-wrenching pain and, praise God, a glorious comeback. Writing this book was an emotional roller coaster. At times, my heart would race, and I felt sick as I revisited the horror of all we went through. At some level, I felt like I was reliving the past, so I really had to dig deep to keep going. I felt vulnerable and wrestled with anxiety, because I've never told anyone the details of everything that happened when Justin was deep in addiction. Even my husband, our children, family, and closest friends, would be coming into most of this information for the very first time as they read this book.

Just the idea of others reading my darkest times filled me with fear, so, whenever I panicked, which happened frequently, I would talk to someone who loves the Lord like I do, and they would remind me that He will bless this writing. This book is not so much about what our family went through, as it is about glorifying the Lord. If our testimony can help others, then we need to tell our story, and that was our focus. Justin kept reminding me to turn to scripture for encouragement, and in one particular conversation he shared Paul's words in 2 Corinthians 1:4 (NLT) "He comforts us in all our troubles so that we can comfort others. When they are troubled, we will be able to give them the same comfort God has given us."

As Justin read me this scripture, it gave me confidence that we were doing the right thing; God will use our suffering for good. I have no doubts.

Now that our story has been told, I realize that God was healing me as I wrote. He was healing my heart in ways I didn't even realize I needed to be healed, and I'm so grateful. Justin and I had daily talks about his life on the streets. I learned a lot about what he went through, and he learned what it was like for me, and I think it was good for both of us. Dillon and I had talks as well, and it seems to have brought our family closer, and made us stronger. Yet, before this writing, we never really talked about all that happened; I think we were so ready for happier days that we didn't want to look back, but sometimes you just need to. When you suffer like we did, you can't forget it ever happened; you must work through it, and we did work through it.

As I dug into our story, I realized the importance of being honest and completely transparent. If the point was to help others, then I knew I had to include everything, no matter how ugly and embarrassing it was. Admittedly, every single day in Justin's addiction was a struggle for me. Anyone that has walked this journey with a loved one knows that it's about survival; you get through each day as best you can.

I know why Justin turned to drugs—he was searching to fill a need that could only be filled in Christ. As I reflected on their childhood, it became clearer than ever what contributed to the pent-up anger and pressure both the boys were feeling. The divorce was a long, hard battle and everyone lost. We all felt it, but the boys were in the middle of it all, and that was tough on them. And I can see that they did not have the right tools to deal with failure and rejection. Justin had an inflated sense of himself; he defined his worth by his performance. So, when life slammed him against the wall and he lost everything, he wasn't equipped to handle it.

I did my best to teach my sons everything they needed to know, but I did not teach them to be like Jesus. I missed that part because I didn't know any better. I hate that I missed that part! Had I been walking in faith, the conversations I would have been having with my sons would have sounded a lot different. I would have been helping them understand where our hope and strength lies. I would have reminded them that mistakes do not define you, and that sports are something you play, but they're not who you are. I would have helped them establish a foundation on which to live, a foundation in Christ. That would have helped Justin immensely, but would it have saved him from becoming a drug addict? I don't know, but I recognize God's perfect timing and how he teaches us in our brokenness. My entire family is stronger because of all that we went through and now, as men, my sons have the wisdom to raise their families on the foundation of Christ and for that, I am eternally grateful.

About addiction, initially I viewed it and the inability to quit as a sign of weakness, but I've since learned a lot. Addiction is a complex issue, and there are lots of different opinions and stigmas attached to it. One of my hopes is that the stigma changes, so those who suffer with addiction are more comfortable reaching out for help. No one chooses to become addicted, but once you're in it, at some point there must be a choice for recovery.

People in addiction that have some clean time and a clear mind have to make a choice to stay clean, or they will continue to relapse. That "stinking thinking" happens when they believe they can handle just one beer, one pill, or one more high. Justin was not successful after rehabs, because rehab was not what he needed. Rehab just brought him back to where he was before drugs, and eventually, he would go back to his same habits—every single time. What he needed was a complete transformation and new life. The Mission House provided the space and support, and then God worked on his heart and he was transformed.

I do believe that those who suffer in addiction can get clean and sometimes stay clean in treatment centers, but Justin could not. He needed to fill the need he kept chasing, and that need was only filled when he found Jesus. Honestly, at some point in life I think most people will find themselves chasing a need; trying to fill up something that is empty inside. Some people try to fill that need with drugs; some people fill it with food, work, porn, control, alcohol, unhealthy relationships, obsessing about their bodies, and so on. The list is endless. Christ made a way to fill Justin and me with peace and love, and it ended our search; we found all we needed in Christ, and so have millions of others. Even though mine and Justin's journeys were completely different, we were both freed in Christ.

People that know me would often comment on my "tough love" strategy with Justin, and let me tell you, it was not a strategy; it was pure instincts and action taken out of total desperation. Watching my son destroy himself was the hardest thing I've ever endured, so I did what I had to do to get through it.

As I reflect on my experience and the choices I made, there's a lot of things I would have done differently, but when addiction hits your family, you just do your best. Addiction is a widespread issue, and there are a lot of resources to help families; you just have to be willing to seek them out.

Below are some of my views about caring for someone in

addiction. Please note that my opinions are based on my family and our experiences. Addiction and family dynamics are complex, and I recognize that what worked for our family may not work for others. My best advice is to ALWAYS seek support!

- If your loved one is actively using, I don't believe you should have them in your home. Until they are ready to get help, nothing seems to work. Trust is a huge issue in addiction and when they're using, they will typically lie and try to manipulate people and situations. Drugs sometimes change people to the extent that they can become almost unrecognizable. Kicking a loved one out of your home can be tough and means they might end up on the street, hungry and cold—which is scary to think about. It's also scary when drug dealers come to your house to collect on a drug debt. Living in all the chaos that typically comes with addiction is ugly and unpredictable, so you've got to establish good boundaries to keep you and your family safe.

- We as parents should not make their lives comfortable. If you are in the "drug life," you cannot come to my home and eat, shower, and sleep. If you are actively using, you're going to live the life of addiction in its full form until you are ready to get help.

- Jail. I would not bail out my loved one who is arrested for anything drug-related.

- Paying Debts. Initially I paid for many things for my son when he was in his addiction, until I realized what I was dealing with. I went through a lot of money, and, if I had known more at the time, I wouldn't have done it. Part of that was my ignorance in not realizing it was going to be a long, five-year struggle. My advice is to not pay for anything that has to do with drugs. They need to dig themselves out of their own messes; otherwise, they'll just keep making the same mistakes, and you'll keep cleaning up after them. I believe it is important for individuals to feel the consequences of their actions.

- When they are ready to get clean, move mountains! Drive, fly, do whatever it takes to get them help. I would do anything for Justin when he was ready to make a change and get clean. If they go to a program and leave before it's over, try to remember that every single day they are clean is a good day. If they can get some clarity for one single day, then that is progress.

- How many times should we foot the bill for a program? That's a tough question. I've known people that had resources and would pay $35,000 or more for a drug treatment center, and it ended up being more like a spa to detox in, and typically the loved one would go right back to using. I did not have the resources and only paid for a plane ticket and $500 to get Justin into The Mission House. The programs up until The Mission House were either free or covered by my insurance. I did pay for detox every time and would have continued to do that. You just have to use your best judgment. The reality is if they're not ready, it doesn't matter what program they go into; it's not going to work. But if they are willing, and you can help them, then I say do it within reason.

When your loved one is ready to get clean, they will find a way, even if you don't help them. Many who struggle in addiction have no support and find their recovery in free/low-cost programs. Lots of programs require participants to work and pay for their stay, and that is a good thing. There is never any guarantee of sobriety, and I would be leery of any program that makes promises of recovery.

- I know what some of you are thinking. What if my actions or inactions hurt my loved one, and he/she

243

ends up dead? My response to that is I understand, it's awful and you will second guess yourself, but there is no prescribed way to do this, and every case is different. Every person is different. If your loved one is using drugs to the extent that they have become addicted and are spiraling out of control, they are already at risk of death. They could be one high away from dying of an overdose, and that can happen on the street or in your own home. Unfortunately, you can't talk someone into getting off drugs; they have to figure it out for themselves.

I believe if someone is deep in their addiction and living the chaotic life that often goes with it, then anything you do to make them more comfortable is just prolonging their demise or rock bottom. If they have money, shelter, a shower, phone, and a car, why would they stop using? You should not always be there to pick up the pieces, because they will come to expect it and take you down with them. Many will disagree with me but that is my opinion. My son's journey was extreme, and as bad as it was, there is something more terrifying about the addict that just uses enough to not crash and ends up living their entire lives in bondage and addicted to drugs.

If your loved one is clean and sober and needs help, help them. Show up for them. Do what is reasonable but be careful and keep good boundaries. Once they're clean, there is a natural course in life, and your adult son or daughter needs to learn to function in this world and make a living on their own and become independent. Help them, support them, love them, but try not to enable them, and don't take over. Keep a healthy distance. Give them a hand-up, not a handout. Pray for them and speak truth, and please, don't make them feel any more ashamed than they already do. Don't bring up the past, trust me they think about the past every day. Our mistakes and past do not define us. We need to lift up those that are suffering and love them.

In closing, I want to be clear on something. I do believe in recovery programs and that people that suffer in addiction can get clean and live a dignified and good life, and I also believe that there is only one Way, one Truth, and one Life, and Jesus Christ is all three. I am convicted in my belief, as I have been witness to the enemy, and I have seen the Lord's favor and miracles, and now, I am unapologetically a believer!

Friends, no matter what you are going through, please don't give up! My beautiful sister-in-Christ, Rosemary, who is one of the godliest women I know, has always told me, "Where there is breath, there is hope," and it's true. I didn't think Justin would make it, but he did. He reached out for help and turned to the Lord.

If we rely on ourselves and our flesh, we will fail, but if our hope and strength lie in the Lord, then anything is possible. My favorite scripture says it best. Proverbs 3:5-6 (NLT) says, "Trust in the Lord with all your heart; do not depend on your own understanding. Seek His will in all you do, and he will show you which path to take."

Seek Him in all my friends; lay your worries at the feet of Christ and pray without ceasing. When you are in need, cry out to the Lord, and He will answer. He always answers because He is sovereign and faithful, and we can stand firmly on His promises.

May God bless the broken. I pray that all who are in the shackles of sin will look up and see the light of the Father that loves us more than we can ever imagine, and it is my hope and prayer that we will all be freed in Christ.

ABOUT THE AUTHOR

Counting Spoons is Kathryn Inman's debut book—but she plans on writing more. Kathryn is a lover of Jesus, nature, and all things beautiful. She currently lives in California with her husband, Darwin. Their growing, blended family includes five adult children, two daughter-in-laws, one soon-to-be son-in-law, and three perfect grandkids.

KATHRYN'S FAMILY

At the time of this publication, Justin and his wife Amanda, their precious daughter Everly Grace, son, Jeremiah Dean, and their big, rambunctious dog Rex, live in Washington. Justin and Amanda both live their life on the foundation of Christ, seeking Him first in all things. They plan on expanding their family and serving the Lord every opportunity they have. Justin continues to thrive in his work, and the future of his family looks bright. In August 2021, Justin celebrated six years of sobriety; well, honestly, Justin didn't celebrate because he doesn't keep track of the time; he only focuses on the present. Kathryn, however, continues to count the days, months, and years of her son's sobriety. Praise Jesus!

Aunt Martha and Uncle Ed live in Castro Valley, California. Martha continues to help edit Kathryn's writing and has her own business, DRIFT Plants ~ a plant shop in California. Martha and Ed love the Lord and are both enjoying life and doing what they do best, making the lives of others a bit more beautiful with plants.

KATHRYNMINMAN.COM

JUSTIN AND
KATHRYN
ENJOYING THE
SUNSHINE
AND WORKING
ON COUNTING
SPOONS!

Kona, Hawaii
January, 2019

SEVEN YEAR
OLD JUSTIN
WITH KATHRYN
AT THE ROLLER
SKATING RINK
PHOTO BOOTH
- TREASURED
MOMENTS.

JUSTIN WITH DAUGHTER EVERLY GRACE
- LOVE CONQUERS ALL!
Christmas, 2020

KATHRYN AND JUSTIN AFTER HIS GRADUATION
FROM THE MISSION HOUSE - FREEDOM!
2016 Port Orchard, Washington

KATHRYN AND JUSTIN - BAPTISM IN THE OCEAN - TEEN CHALLEGE
PROGRAM IN SOUTHERN CALIFORNIA. TAKING ONE DAY AT A TIME.

JUSTIN
AFTER
HIS FIRST
THIRTY-DAY
REHAB. A
LONG, HARD
ROAD IS
AHEAD.

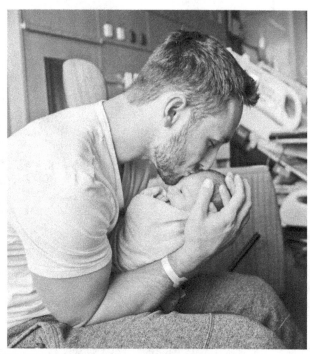

A MESSAGE FROM JUSTIN

It's a cool, crisp evening here in the Pacific Northwest. Nothing but clear skies and mountains stretching out as far as you can see. I button up my coat as the chill sets in and decide it's time to head back from our after-dinner walk. My daughter sings softly as she twirls about, never letting go of my hand. My son kicks his little feet against the stroller, keeping his eyes on Rex, our faithful dog who trots ahead of us, wagging his tail in excitement. As we make our way up the path, the sun dips below the clouds and illuminates brightly through every window in our home. I pause at the beauty of it and fight back my tears. God has blessed me richly. I see my beautiful, God-loving wife waiting at our front door, smiling. I look down at our precious children and perfect dog standing beside me. I have a steady income, a comfortable home, food on the table, reliable cars, and the list goes on. It's hard to believe that just six years ago, I was a homeless drug addict chasing my next high. I once had an intimate relationship with Christ until my pride caused me to stray, then the Father's love drew me back. I stop to soak in the sweetness of life in this very moment, and my thoughts drift to Ephesians 2:4 (ESV).

"But God, who is rich in mercy, because of His great love with which He loved us, even when we were dead in trespasses, made us alive together with Christ (by grace you have been saved)."

Material possessions are not the substance of my joy and freedom—Christ is. Comforts of life are simply a reminder of God's grace and mercy. Where I came from, and how the Lord saved me, is what stirs my spirit to pursue Christ. I want to stay humble and broken before the Lord. I want the little things, like a walk with my children, to always remind me of the overwhelming goodness of Jesus.

The Greek word for "remember" is tattooed on my left forearm. Revelations 2:5 states "remember the heights to which you have fallen." The placement on my arm was intentional—it covers scars I have from shooting dope. This tattoo is my daily reminder to pause and thank the Lord for rescuing me. Please, my friends, for the sake of Christ, remember where your sin led you and where Christ saved you. I, for one, will never forget.